Taking a Break
from Saving the World

Taking a Break from Saving the World

A Conservation Activist's Journey
from Burnout to Balance

By Stephen Legault

RMB

For information on purchasing bulk quantities of this book, or to obtain media excerpts or invite the author to speak at an event, please visit rmbooks.com and select the "Contact" tab.

RMB | Rocky Mountain Books Ltd.
rmbooks.com
@rmbooks
facebook.com/rmbooks

Cataloguing data available from Library and Archives Canada
ISBN 9781771603638 (paperback)
ISBN 9781771603645 (electronic)

Printed and bound in Canada

We would like to also take this opportunity to acknowledge the traditional territories upon which we live and work. In Calgary, Alberta, we acknowledge the Niitsitapi (Blackfoot) and the people of the Treaty 7 region in Southern Alberta, which includes the Siksika, the Piikuni, the Kainai, the Tsuut'ina and the Stoney Nakoda First Nations, including Chiniki, Bearpaw, and Wesley First Nations. The City of Calgary is also home to Métis Nation of Alberta, Region III. In Victoria, British Columbia, we acknowledge the traditional territories of the Lkwungen (Esquimalt, and Songhees), Malahat, Pacheedaht, Scia'new, T'Sou-ke and W̱SÁNEĆ (Pauquachin, Tsartlip, Tsawout, Tseycum) peoples.

We acknowledge the financial support of the Government of Canada through the Canada Book Fund and the Canada Council for the Arts, and of the province of British Columbia through the British Columbia Arts Council and the Book Publishing Tax Credit.

Disclaimer
The views expressed in this book are those of the author and do not necessarily reflect those of the publishing company, its staff or its affiliates.

For Jenn,
For Silas and Rio,
For the Belly River,
Guides on the journey downstream.

Contents

Author's Caution

Everything in this book may be wrong.
It's offered with the best of intent,
but it's personal opinion
and may be out in left field.

You've been warned.

Preface

To burn out you must once have been on fire.

—UNKNOWN[1]

This is a book about what can happen when we spend our lives trying to make the world a better place but overlook taking care of ourselves. People who are deeply engaged in the good work of saving the world[2] – regardless of how grand or humble our efforts – can at times suffer from an inability to remain resilient. In plain speak, we burn out.[3]

If we're employed in the nonprofit sector, this can lead to serious problems that can impact our careers. We may feel compelled to quit, we may get fired when our work suffers, and we may suffer from physical or emotional health problems.

Despite increasing efforts by the organizations in the nonprofit sector, when staff burn out it can feel as if we are on our own. As the voluntary sector is often working right at the margins of its capacity to sustain itself, when one of our team suffers burnout, the result can be a transfer of the workload, and its accompanying anxiety, to other teammates.

As volunteers and grassroots activists, burning out can ultimately have the same outcome, but we may receive even *less* support from the causes and groups we serve. The consequences can be very serious. The rate of suicide among people who identify as social-profit employees or volunteers has long been a point of concern. While statistics aren't available to compare the rate of suicide among activists with those in greater society, numerous anecdotal examples exist.[4]

"This field is so full of depression and stress and negativity and suicide," says Dr. Jim Butler, professor emeritus at the University of Alberta in Edmonton. "In fact, this field has one of the highest suicide rates of any field, you'd be interested to know. Most people do it in the form of outdoor accidents so that the insurance goes back to the family or causes that they care about. I could give you a long list of people whose friends know that was the case."[5] Dr. Butler delivered these remarks at the inaugural conference of the Yellowstone to Yukon Conservation Initiate (Y2Y) at Waterton Lakes National Park in the fall of 1997. I was the chair of that conference.

I've heard Dr. Butler deliver this message a few times in the more than 20 years since that September day in Waterton. I'm always astonished to look around the room at the number of heads nodding, and the tears in listeners' eyes.

In a March 2018 *New York Times* piece, John Eligon investigated the high rate of premature death among founders and activists from the Black Lives Matter movement. "With each fallen comrade, activists are left to ponder their own mortality and whether the many pressures of the movement contributed to the shortened lives of their colleagues."[6]

"I'm skilled at eluding the fetal crouch of despair – because I've been working on climate change for thirty years," says author and activist Bill McKibben in the *New Yorker* magazine. "I've learned to parcel out my angst, to keep my distress under control. But, in the past few months, I've more often found myself awake at night with true fear-for-your-kids anguish."[7] McKibben, who has led the fight against climate change for 30 years, says that, despite the efforts of millions to address the climate crisis, the angst of emergency often wakes him at 2 a.m. to worry about our collective future.

Long-term physical or mental health issues can and have sidelined some of the most promising activists striving for social change. This can have a lasting impact on their ability to live fulfilling, healthy and rewarding lives. Aside from the personal impact of these challenges, the impact of burnout and its outcomes can be challenging for the management of the organizations that are striving to make the world better. Loss of productive labour hours, high staff turnover, low morale and toxicity in the workplace all take their toll. The cost to recruit and train new staff, and the significant loss of institutional memory, can be significant obstacles to the success of social-profit organizations.

People come and go from organizations that serve the cause of social or environmental justice, humanitarian needs or peace, just as they do in more traditional forms of employment. There is conflicting data on the rate of employee turnover in the nongovernmental organization (NGO) sector, however.[8]

According to the Society for Human Resources Management's *2016 Human Capital Benchmarking Report*, turnover in the nonprofit sector is the exact same – 19 per cent – as in the for-profit sector.[9] Most managers in the NGO sector might be surprised to read that our turnover is so low; it feels like we're always short of staff and bleeding talent. There is contradictory evidence on the rate of turnover in nonprofit organizations, just as there are other factors at play.

"Non-profits tend to 'run on tired,'" says Tracy Vanderneck, president of Phil-Com, a Florida-based consulting firm. "They may have too few staff members doing too many jobs and always feel like they are behind. Because of this, the organization's leadership spends their time putting out fires instead of proactively putting a solid plan in place for recruitment, training and continual stewarding of employees."[10]

Maybe all four of your four staff positions are filled, but you are trying to do the work of eight or 12 people.

The contrast to this comes from Mario Siciliano, who as president and CEO of Volunteer Calgary in 2008 noted, "Turnover in the non-profit sector is very high. Lately in Alberta, it is estimated to be between 30% and 40%. We also know that the non-profit sector has one of the highest rates of applications for long-term disability because of stress." Siciliano says, "[There is] no doubt it is there. When you combine a critical lack of resources with people who are so passionate about the work they are doing; they don't want to stop. It is a recipe for stress and burnout."[11]

Just as the rate of turnover fluctuates with the employment rate, location and general economic trends, the rate specific to nonprofits also fluctuates. While turnover rates are one indicator of nonprofit health, so are the statistics around overall mental health in the workforce. "A recent Gallup study of nearly 7,500 full-time employees found that 23 percent reported feeling burned out at work very often or always, while an additional 44 percent reported feeling burned out sometimes," reported CNBC in August of 2018.[12]

The personal crisis, and the crisis facing the nonprofit sector, is not likely to get any better. The new energy injected into the climate emergency through student-led strikes, the Green New Deal and the debate over climate change as a dominant issue in the politics of many countries worldwide has attracted a new generation of activists. Some, like those who identify themselves as the Sunrise Movement, are young, well educated and racially diverse. They are, according to *Vox Online*, "young, angry, and effective."[13]

Thirty years ago that line might have been used to describe my efforts to raise awareness of many of the same issues the Sunrise Movement seeks to highlight today, though how effective my colleagues and I were is open for debate. Nearly everybody I joined arms with during those early days of my life as an activist continues to work for social change today. Many, however, have suffered the consequences of overwork, commitment and burnout.

If I could say one thing to the new generation of activists – from the Sunrise Movement to Black Lives Matter to Idle No More – it would be this: it's a marathon, not a sprint. To survive such an endurance race as we face in the effort to address the climate emergency, inequality and the myriad crises of our generation, we have to pace ourselves. If we don't, we run the risk of great personal challenges, and we won't be around continuing the struggle we feel so passionately about now.

While our organizations have an important role to play in addressing burnout and its consequences, it's at the personal level that each member of the global activist community can make a difference. Learning to stay healthy as an activist often runs contrary to the self-sacrificing nature of those who are compelled to make the world a better place.

I am saying that sometimes we have to take a break from saving the world. Once in a while, regardless of how important our work is – and the role it plays in defining the story of our own lives – we have to eddy out.

To "eddy out" is a phrase coined by canoeists, kayakers and other river runners. When you're paddling a river – especially one with rapids and other obstacles – sometimes you need to take a break in order to rest, scout the way forward or just appreciate the majesty of moving water. Unlike with a lake, you can't just pull over to the shore or drift quietly on calm waters; the current keeps pulling you downriver.

To take a break you have to look for an eddy – a spot on the inside bank of the river where a rock, or some other obstruction, creates a sheltered section of water where the current is calm or reverses direction and moves back upriver.

The place where the water reverses course is called the "eddy line," or sometimes the eddy fence. To cut the eddy fence, you aim the bow (the front) of your boat into the top of the eddy. The paddler in the stern (back) of the boat paddles so the boat turns sharply while the paddler in the bow digs in to keep the boat's momentum. If you do it right, the boat swings gracefully around and you find yourself in quiet water. If you mess it up, you might get swept downstream, sideways or backwards. Sometimes, if the eddy fence is particularly rough, you can capsize.

This is analogous to my own metaphorical experience eddying out.

For most paddlers, however, it usually goes well, and once in the eddy you can rest on quiet water as the river rushes by. This can provide a much needed rest on a big river, and gives you a chance to even step out of the boat to scout downstream for rapids, hazards and more good clean fun.

THE COST OF CAPSIZING

Capsizing – burning out, quitting, getting canned – has an institutional cost and a personal one. The forfeiture of human potential at the individual level is one of the greatest, and least discussed, costs of being forced out or voluntarily leaving an organization. "The earth needs you and if you burn out, it will not have you," reminds Jim Butler.[14]

The real capital that fuels the nonprofit sector is passion. The people who make up the ranks of grassroots volunteers, staff and leaders of this sector have extraordinary potential to change the world. The sidelining of that potential due to burnout may be one critical factor that determines if we are ultimately successful in our efforts to make the world a better place.

Life is a remarkable gift and the idea of squandering it, or not being able to rise to our greatest calling, is a tragedy. We all have the potential to create something positive, even if it's as simple but meaningful as how we express kindness to those around us. Identifying the barriers that keep us from our potential, and addressing the systemic reasons for this with clear-sighted solutions, is one of the most important aspects of leadership in the world of the nonprofit sector.

When I took my first formal leadership job as executive director of Wildcanada.net in 1999, I was 28 years old. Up until that point, most of my training in leadership had come from volunteer positions with clubs or as a member of boards of directors. While leading Wildcanada.net, I encouraged and tried to support my small team to develop a set of goals related to what they wanted to get out of their work experience, besides a paycheque. Good work, meaningful employment or volunteer undertakings can help people achieve the highest aims in human existence – to find meaning and live with less suffering and experience self-actualization.

I wasn't well prepared to support my team at Wildcanada.net in this way. Learning how to support our team so they don't burn out is part of a cultural shift that has been underway for some time in the nonprofit sector, but we still have a long way to go. I'll examine this cultural shift in Chapter 9 of this book.

People don't come to volunteer or work in the social-profit sector because they believe that everything is just peachy, thank you. They gravitate to organizations that have a mandate to address climate change or poverty or famine because they are impacted by the conditions of suffering in the world themselves. Good, meaningful work, done well and in balance with life's other priorities, can be deeply cathartic.

It can also have the exact opposite of its intended effect on those doing the work.

Taking a Break from Saving the World is a short manifesto told from my own 30-year experience in the cause-related workforce. The book is intended to be both practical and inquisitive. I want you to come away with some ideas that you can apply in your work and life immediately, while giving you something to think about that helps frame our quest for greater purpose and meaning through good work.

The first two chapters of this book examine the causes of burnout in the nonprofit sector, how we can manage our time and energy in a way that allows us to stay in our boats longer and how to identify the signs that our stress levels are becoming dangerous. I'll examine some of the reasons why employees and volunteers in the nonprofit sector capsize when it comes to long-term resilience, and how to stay in the boat longer.

Chapter 3 looks at the question of when to eddy out. When is it time to take a break from saving the world, and what might we expect when we do? I'll suggest some of the things you can do if you no longer think the work you are doing is serving you or your cause, and how to know when it's time to quit. I'll also examine what to expect, and what to do, if you get fired.

Chapters 4 and 5 examine in detail how to cut the eddy fence if we've decided it's time.

In Chapter 6 – "Thrown Overboard" – I'll write about my own experience losing my job in the conservation movement, and some things to consider if your own stress and anxiety cause work-related challenges that may lead to your dismissal.

Regardless of how you ended up in an eddy, we consider what to do when you are safely in quiet water, reading the river and its path forward. This will be in Chapter 7. In Chapters 8 and 9 we'll point our bow back into the main current and consider how to prepare ourselves for the wild ride to come. This will include a look at our organizations and institutions and how they can better support our efforts to stay healthy.

There are more than 100,000 people employed in the NGO sector in North America. Another two million people volunteer for NGOs across the continent. The vast majority of these people are everyday, average Canadians and Americans, doing their best to make the world a better place.

Some of them serve food at homeless shelters, some help storm-damaged communities clean up after disasters; others help restore habitat along damaged stream banks. Many people in the NGO sector do this because they care deeply and passionately about people, their communities and the planet. The vast majority have regular jobs in addition to their efforts to save the world.

I've been trying to save the world since I started my high school's recycling club in 1988. Since then, I've served on half a dozen boards of directors for conservation groups, helped start two national or international conservation organizations, and worked with more than two dozen businesses and nonprofits on issues like youth employment, children's mental health, homelessness and poverty reduction. My own personal observation of the NGO sector, from inside as a volunteer or staff person, as an external organizational development consultant, and based on studies of the sector conducted by numerous independent researchers, is that it is too often troubled with leadership that's more focused on external objectives than internal team health. Our strategies for addressing these problems are ineffective and fail to sustain the well-being of our workforce. We need to make significant improvements if we're going to overcome the obstacles we face.

Later in the manifesto, when I address institutional opportunities for course correction and suggest that maybe we are *too* focused on building long-lasting organizations, the notion of long-term viability will seem like a contradiction. In a way, it is; if we're *going* to have lasting organizations, then we must take better care of our people. We also need less *organizational* building and more individual enablement – empowering people to make change. Creating health within the workforce of the organization builds an inherent and resilient strength that is projected outwards to achieve its objectives.

Despite these significant challenges to resilience, the NGO sector continues to grow and do extraordinary work.

The pressure of saving the world is at times overwhelming and can lead to breakdowns in people's personal lives, their withdrawal from long-term participation in the voluntary sector and serious risks to their physical and mental health, including the risk of suicide. Facing overwhelming challenges such as climate change, natural disasters, famine, disease, poverty and the loss of biodiversity can at times feel crushing.

Despite this, the NGO sector is one of the fastest growing workforces in North America.[15] According to the US Bureau of Labor Statistics, the nonprofit sector is the third-largest employer in the United States behind manufacturing and retail. In Canada, the nonprofit workforce is the second largest, proportionally, in the world behind the Netherlands. Twelve per cent of the country's workforce is in the nonprofit sector.[16]

There are plenty of reports and articles about how to manage stress in the workforce and how to address the anxiety and depression that can emerge from cause-based work. We'll consider these in Chapter 2, but I encourage you to dig much deeper to discover your own way of "staying above water."

One of the side effects of the taxing nature of the work in the NGO sector is the need to eddy out. To step out, take a break and learn how to manage the pressure of saving the world. Typically, there are three ways this might happen: we can quit, we can burn out or we can get fired. These three means of stepping out can occur in various combinations. You might burn out and quit, or you might burn out and get fired. Or you might burn out and persist, and, in doing so, create serious challenges for yourself, your family and your organization. These obstacles might be physical symptoms of stress that can span a wide range of short- and long-term illnesses, or they might be emotional symptoms related to anxiety, depression and contemplating suicide.

There is a fourth way we can respond to the pressure that arises from our efforts to make the world a better place: we can eddy out. We might come to understand the difficulty inherent in the work we do, and adjust both our proactive approach and response to it to avoid the pitfalls that lead to quitting, burning out or being fired. We can build in resilience tools and create the physical and emotional space needed to sustain ourselves in the stressful work of the voluntary sector in a way that allows us to gain perspective and then opt to get back on the river when we're ready.

This manifesto is dedicated to three simple ideas. The first is to learn when and how to eddy out, regardless of our particular circumstances. The second is to explore what to do when we find ourselves in the comparatively quiet waters of an eddy. Finally, we'll look at when, and how, to eddy back in.

Notes on Technique

At the end of each chapter of *Taking a Break* I'll make a few notes on how to get the most out of that particular section of the book. I'm calling these "Notes on Technique" to fit with the theme of a paddling guide. Here are a few things to consider:

1. You likely got into the particular boat you're in right now – the conservation movement, social justice or equality movements, humanitarian work – for very complex reasons. Sometimes we're compelled by the suffering of the world to grab a paddle. Sometimes the thing we love the most is threatened. Other times we're looking for a way to fit into the world and jumping into a cause and paddling like hell seems like a good way to do it. Consider why you are in the boat you are in.

2. Make notes. Scribble all over this book. Make one hell of a mess.

3. Consider making commitments to yourself, and with someone else who can help hold you accountable to those commitments. Find a buddy and read together.

4. Be gentle with yourself. Some of the reasons this work is so hard is because we're all suffering a little (or a lot), and it's impossible for most of us to separate that from our work. In fact, in many cases it's what makes us compassionate toward the suffering of others.

5. Finally, you likely won't get this "right" the first time. I'm starting my fourth go-round, and will likely botch this up too, so accept this as an iterative learning experience, just like everything else in life.

Chapter 1

Paddling Heavy Water

I'm going to start by telling you a little bit of my own story to provide context for the rest of this short book. During my most recent full-time employment, for an international conservation organization called the Yellowstone to Yukon Conservation Initiative, I got fired. It wasn't the first time I'd lost a job, but it was the most difficult dismissal of my professional career, and it was the motivation for writing this book.

I got fired from Parks Canada in the mid-1990s after publicly embarrassing the regional director at a staff meeting by asking a question she didn't like.[17] I got fired from my first writing gig at the *Banff Crag & Canyon* when advertisers complained I was antidevelopment. And in 2009 I got laid off from Royal Roads University during the stock market crash.

I've also burned out before, like when I capsized the boat while leading Wildcanada.net in the mid-2000s. I gave 18 months notice that I was leaving that job, but not before getting good and crispy and making a hash of things on both the home front and at work. My relationship and the organization didn't survive.[18]

After leaving Wildcanda.net in 2006 I took a hiatus from full-time conservation efforts for almost five years. I ran a consulting business that catered to nonprofit organizations, social-profit businesses and governments. In 2010 I returned to Alberta from Victoria, BC, and took a position with the organization I had helped get off the ground. My employment with Y2Y between 2011 and 2018 was intense and all-consuming, and I let it get the better of me. I didn't eddy out.

My involvement with Y2Y dated back to 1996 when I first joined the group's fledgling steering committee and acted as the volunteer chair of our Connections Conference in 1997. At that time, I was just barely making ends meet working for a tiny conservation research firm in Banff, Alberta, and volunteering nearly full-time for the Alberta Wilderness Association, along with other grass-roots groups.

I spent nearly five years as the coordinator of the Crown Conservation Initiative (CCI), a collaborative effort of regional conservation organizations, land trusts and academic institutions working on landscape conservation and climate change, and hosted by Y2Y.

From 2015 through July 2018, I was the program director for Alberta, the Crown of the Continent and the Northwest Territories. During that time I made a lot of mistakes and got a few things right, and, in doing so, learned a great deal. What I know beyond a reasonable doubt is how important it is for us in the nonprofit sector to safeguard our own well-being and that of our teammates.

The people I've worked with – and there are hundreds, maybe thousands of them – are extraordinary. Passionate, dedicated and mostly selfless in their pursuit of a better world. One of the things that characterizes activists – and maybe this is what draws us together – is that we're a little unbalanced in the first place. Workaholics, obsessives, perfectionists and myopic, we have dedicated ourselves to a cause and are relentless, sometimes regardless of the cost.

There are plenty of us who actually suffer from genuine emotional or mental health issues. Some of us became activists because of damage we'd already sustained and were looking for a path with meaning to try and create some balance in our lives. Others of us joined a cause because it was a way of blanketing our illnesses under altruism or ego. Others still have been run into the ground by the pressure and despair that comes when facing some of the world's most pressing challenges.

I'm all three. I grew up with an alcoholic mother whose approval I sought constantly but would never fully receive. When I was 16, my parents divorced, and I sought sanctuary in the woods behind my home in Burlington, Ontario, only to witness their destruction as a highway was punched through my refuge. I took up the cause of environmental activism, and it quickly made me a big fish in the small pond that is high school and, later, college.

We all have our reasons for doing what we do. Most of us have the very best interests of the planet, its wild critters and that of humanity as a motivation. But let's not kid ourselves: many of us are trying to heal deep wounds, and our efforts to save the world are a part of that.

This is important because it underscores the context of this little book. Sometimes in order to be effective in our efforts to make the world a better place, we have to eddy out.

I had some notice that my dismissal from Y2Y was likely. I was put on probation in April of 2018, and in the months between that notification and my ultimate exit from the organization I had a lot of time to think and fret about my circumstances. I had even reached the uneasy decision that, rather than waiting around to be dismissed, I would quit on my own. That decision was made while camping on the banks of the Belly River in Waterton Lakes National Park, a place that has long held deep spiritual and emotional reverence for my family and me.

What became apparent as Jenn and I talked long into the night that July long weekend in Waterton was that some of the old lessons I thought I'd gleaned from previous experiences needed relearning, and fresh lessons are never in short supply. As the sun slipped behind the peaks that cradled the headwaters of the Belly River, I felt a disease growing at the thought of quitting. My stomach felt sick, like I might vomit, as I contemplated what I was about to do.

I thought to myself: Am I making the right choice? What if this is a mistake? What will I do if I don't succeed? Who will I be without this job, this title and the power that comes with it? But what will I become if I stay? What have I *already* become?

The German philosopher Friedrich Nietzsche said, "Anyone who fights with monsters should take care that he does not in the process become a monster."[19] I can imagine some of those who have criticized my style of activism looking at that quote and wondering, just who do I think is the monster?

We are the monster.

Or, more precisely, we may become the monster if we aren't careful.

"We come back to where we started. 'We have met the enemy and he is us' becomes 'we have met the enemy and he has become us,'" say the authors of *Getting to Maybe: How the World Is Changed.*[20]

Contemplating this on the banks of the Belly River, the water moving so slowly between the tight-fitting banks as to appear still, I wondered if I was worried what I would become, or what I would become *more of*?

I have dedicated my life to the cause of nature conservation. I started my first conservation group when I was 16 years old. That was more than 30 years ago. I began to worry that I might not have all that long left if I didn't eddy out. My mental health was in shambles. My blood pressure was through the roof during my last physical. I couldn't sleep. I was short-tempered. I couldn't remember simple things and had lost much of the perspective gained after leaving Wildcanada.net and penning *Carry Tiger to Mountain* and *Running Toward Stillness*.

My work was not responsible for this. Nor was the structure and demands of the environmental movement in general. There is a shared responsibility between our various movements' leaders and those who strive to make the world a better place to care for one another. The way we do our work, however, and what we expect of each other in the effort to save the world, is certainly complicit and must be addressed.

"There are other causes of stress associated with environmental activism," says Dr. Butler in his talk to the Y2Y conference in Waterton.

> Work has no closure of business hours. You'll identify with all this. It's your life. It's why you feel the stress and why your dog's growling at you. This obsession with keeping informed, staying on top of everything. The truth is, you can't. That's called the Atlas complex, where the fate of the earth is in your hands. It's on your back. Another cause of stress particular to the environmental movement is the emotional vulnerability you experience when what you love is threatened or harmed. You open up to hurt when you love. You face this in individual relationships. When you open your heart to love, you become vulnerable. When you love wilderness and wildlife and wild places, you get hurt. It doesn't mean you close

your heart: you accept that and you know it and it hurts and it's a natural part of all that we do.[21]

LEARNING FROM RIVERS

There is a fat eddy on the Belly River where it sweeps slowly around the grassy bend by the rock beach below the Parks Canada campground. There are beavers in this reach of the river, and mergansers. Sandhill cranes make their nests near these banks and often are seen pacing along the small sandy beaches. The water here turns back on itself, pools and then almost seamlessly rejoins the river's flow. The way the river fits so perfectly between its green banks is a strange and significant comfort.

My family and I have paddled this section of the river in lightweight kayaks, playing in this eddy line, nosing upriver from backwater to backwater eddy, before surrendering to the pull of the river's patient, persistent flow. Silas, my youngest son, has said of this reach: "There isn't a 200-metre stretch of river that I love more." I love it too. I have learned from this reach of the Belly River that sometimes you have to cut the eddy fence and take a break from saving the world.

To eddy out isn't to surrender. It's not retreat. It's not as if in making the decision to step out that I'm leaving the river entirely. I'm simply going to rest in the calm water for a moment. I need to catch my breath. I want to read the river from a vantage point of peace, assess the downstream rapids and plot a course through the rocks. I might even step ashore and scout downstream a bit, but I will always keep the river in sight.

I'm not forsaking the river, I tell myself. I'm just plotting a better course forward.

The evening's doubts fade as the light vanishes from the sky. The horizon over the Beebee Flats – a sacred place for the Blood tribe of the Blackfoot Confederacy and a grounding landscape for my family for a long time now – is bulging with clouds the colour of a ripe plum. Grouse beat the air in the aspens behind us; we can feel the thrum in our chests. Then it is quiet, deliciously so. Even the cool breeze – a katabatic wind slipping down still snowy mountains – feels inviting. It's pulling me forward rather than holding me back.

Jenn and I walk back to our camp, the tall grass brushing our downward-facing palms, her arm wrapped tightly with mine. I know this is the right thing to do. It's time.

Circumstances intervened upon my return to Canmore and the office on Tuesday morning. Before I could get the chance to hand in my resignation, I was dismissed.

And now I wonder: What if there had been another option? The chance to eddy out, rather than burn out, quit or get fired?

Notes on Technique:
Paddling Heavy Water

1. When you're paddling heavy water, you must consider not only the obvious hazards but also those unseen just below the surface of the river. Sweepers, rocks just below the surface and dangerous obstacles in the river might not be visible when you scout a rapid. While observing the big waters and major river hazards, consider what might be hidden that can flip your boat, and prepare accordingly.

2. Now is a good time to consider why you picked up this book in the first place. Maybe you're just getting started in the social-profit world; maybe you've been at this all your life. Maybe it's time to fine-tune some of your efforts to maintain good health while working to save the world. Maybe you're at the end of your rope. What made you pick up this book? What do you want to get out of it?

3. Consider this: Do you already know that it's time to eddy out?

Chapter 2

The High Brace

Let's backpaddle a bit.

The best way to avoid the perils of heavy water is to learn how to keep your boat upright while you're running big waves. Let's face it: everybody who has committed themselves to a cause – poverty relief, climate change, electoral reform – is going to find themselves, from time to time, in prolonged periods of stress. Knowing when to keep paddling and how to navigate these tough waters, and then knowing when to take a break by eddying out, is an important tool for long-term success.

Pete MacDowell, executive director with Democracy South, says this in an article written by Dianne J. Russell: "Unlike most jobs, being an activist is a life cause. You have an attitude that you are saving the Earth and bringing justice. But that's what makes it hard to find a boundary between your work-life and your own life."[22]

Sometimes when running big water, a maneuver is needed to keep the boat from capsizing. There are a number of ways of doing this. One of these is the high brace.

Big water can seem almost solid sometimes. When it comes across the bow of your boat and snaps your head back with its weight, you might swear you were paddling through concrete. This can be used to your advantage. If you feel as though the boat is going over, reach far out – both hands firm on the paddle – and slap the water with the blade. For a moment it will feel as though you can push on the water, and in doing so you can keep your boat upright for another moment. This is called a "high brace" and it's a useful technique to learn.

There are a lot of resources for people who want to keep their boat afloat during difficult times. Workshops abound, and it's hard to go to a training session in the save-the-world sector without some kind of circle forming where we talk honestly about how we're feeling and what can be done to support one another. The elements that are often missing are systematic follow-up, personal commitment and meaningful support from the organization's leadership.

The first and maybe most important aspect to addressing stress, anxiety and the eventual burnout that can stem from these trials is a genuine desire to face the challenge honestly.

Some people don't mind burning out; it's their operational pattern. They work like hell for a few years, or longer, and then crash, burn, dust themselves off and rejoin the fray. These folks must be extra cautious when they find themselves in leadership roles. Having the self-awareness to know that your particular style of addressing the strain of working in the nonprofit sector isn't applicable to everyone is important. Not everybody relishes or has the resilience to withstand bursting into flames every few years. Learning to support teammates in a way that sustains them over time is vital.

Some of us, however, are less overt about our need to burn out. Some of us simply ignore the threat it poses to our individual health, that of our close relations and to our movements. Why would we do this? Martyring ourselves for a cause at least has the benefit of creating some notoriety. "Oh, did you hear about Steph? Yeah, he really burned out. He was so committed…."

It's unlikely that we do this on purpose. Sometimes we just need a way out and the only option is to work ourselves so hard that we're left with no alternative other than to pull the plug. There are alternatives, however, and that's what we're here to explore.

WHY AND HOW TO STAY IN YOUR BOAT

I won't create an exhaustive list here, but some of the reasons not to allow ourselves to be thrown from our boats are to avoid heart attacks, strokes, ulcers, chronic fatigue, sexual dysfunction, dangerous levels of depression and a host of stomach- and digestive-related ailments.

If you don't care so much about your own well-being, consider those who share your life with you. I bet you're a barrel of laughs when you're stressed to the gills and approaching full crispiness. I certainly am! The reality is that when we're suffering from anxiety and stress related to work, we are anything but fun to be around. I'm also not very good at my work when I'm failing in my efforts at resiliency.

So what is your motivation to stay in the boat?

In order to stay in your boat, the first thing you need to consider is this: Do you have a sincere desire to live your life and do your work in a way that is healthy for you and for those around you? Do not martyr yourself. Martyrs make very little actual progress on the things that are important to them because, by definition, they are dead.

The second thing to consider in the effort to do our work in a way that is healthy, and makes actual rather than symbolic progress, is to learn to see the signs of stress and burnout before they overtake you. This is an important point to consider: if you're truly dedicated to your cause, you have an obligation to take care of yourself so you can do your very best work. Ask yourself: Am I in this for the long haul, or am I just going through the motions? "Today, most often, we talk about survival meaning the survival of those who fight for the earth," says Jim Butler. "You and your ability to survive. Your ability to deal with stress and to hold on and to keep your grounding, without inhibiting your spiritual growth and your capacity to really understand the outdoors."[23]

Identifying the signs of stress and burnout before they swamp your boat can be difficult. Take a minute and ask yourself the following questions:

1. When I get up in the morning, do I feel excited about my day, or do I feel a sense of dread?

2. When I'm volunteering, or when I'm at work, do I feel energized by the day's little challenges, or do they easily defeat me?

3. When I'm discussing what I do with others, is my excitement contagious, or do I leave the impression that this effort is hopeless?

4. If I spend a few minutes thinking about my future, and honestly assess my current role, do I feel excited about continuing or wish I were doing something else?

5. How does my body react to my current efforts? Do I most often feel healthy and in tune with my work, or is my body sending me troubling signals such as headaches, upset stomach, pain or ongoing illnesses?

These are, of course, binary options, and the world doesn't really sort itself out so neatly. The point of this sort of reflection is to become aware of our own circumstances and to monitor our physical, mental and emotional health in an honest and ongoing way.

Often it is most difficult to assess these challenges on our own. We tend to wear blinders to our own challenges, while being hypersensitive to the challenges of others. Why not enlist some help? A close friend, a family member or a coworker – one you don't report to or doesn't report to you – may be able to help you answer these questions.

If you're in the nonprofit world, and are starting to feel as if you're approaching a high stress situation, ask your close friends, your partner or a

41

family member to give you feedback. Are they noticing things you do not? Check in often and ask them for the unvarnished truth, and be prepared to hear it.

There are certainly days in even the healthiest work environments when we wake up and think, "I just don't want to do this today," or find ourselves with a backache or shoulder problems from sitting in front of our computers too long. The telling features of serious burnout versus short-term strain are twofold. First, is there a trend in how we answer the questions above, and others, about our own response to work? If you notice that over the course of several months, or a year, you are waking up and dreading what you do, or finding yourselves lacking resolve or the physical stamina to undertake your work, then that's something you must pay attention to.

The second feature is less obvious: Are you able to be honest with yourself? Self-deception is not at all uncommon, but it's a telltale sign that maybe something is amiss. If you're misleading yourself that everything is just fine, and these headaches, or this knot in your stomach, are just you being too sensitive, then you may want to examine that a little more closely. Staying in the boat means having to be brutally honest with yourself that there is, in fact, a problem.

If you're feeling more than just the occasional stress, and the symptoms are pointing toward burnout, there is a range of things you can do to help keep *you* in the boat. First, make a plan.

It doesn't need to be a long plan, but it needs to be specific. What do you need to be healthy and happy?

Here's a few things *I need* that might help you get started:

1. Exercise, lots of it.

2. Meditation.[24]

3. Time outside, away from work, the further away from civilization the better.

4. Opportunities to learn and grow.

5. A healthy diet. (I don't like this one, as I'd rather eat crap and drink beer, but I'm told it's important.)

6. Sleep.

7. Vacations, away from work, with no email or phone calls, preferably with my wife and kids.

8. Support for the above from my supervisor. And here I don't mean just verbal support but actual organizational support. Don't tell me I need to get more sleep, or exercise, or a nice long vacation, and then schedule me for a staff retreat when I'm supposed to be away with my family, or pile a dozen grant applications on my desk and tell me they're due Friday.

9. A willingness to take responsibility for the things that keep me healthy, regardless of whether or not I get the above described support.

Making a Plan

From time to time in *Taking a Break*, I'll suggest you make a plan. I have a bit of a complicated relationship with plans. I love them but also think they're relatively useless. As they say, "No plan survives first contact with the enemy." As we're also the "enemy" in this case (the enemy of our own happiness and sense of fulfillment), that won't take very long.

The purpose of almost any plan is to become accustomed to the process of thinking critically. Here are some things to consider when I suggest making a plan:

- Write it down. Keep it handy to refer to on a daily or regular basis.

- Share it with someone you trust. Maybe this is the person you have asked to monitor your efforts, or, maybe, as I'll discuss later, it's your personal board of directors.

- Make it specific, time-bound and scalable. Saying I'm going to eat well and exercise doesn't help; saying I'm going to cut out donuts and start going to the gym four days a week is better.

- Keep it simple. One page will do. Use bullets (there's no need for lengthy paragraphs).

Make your own list. Write this list down and hold yourself to it. Ask a friend, a partner or a colleague to help keep you accountable to these commitments.[25]

Despite the best-laid plans, revised often and supported by friends, family and co-workers, sometimes, when we're in heavy water, we're going to take some waves over the bow. We need to be vigilant. Here's a partial list of challenges to keep an eye out for, and a few ideas on what you can do to address these difficult issues:

Challenges	Possible Solutions
Are you getting enough sleep?	If not, try cutting down on caffeine, especially after noon, getting more exercise and avoiding screens of any kind right before bed. *Never* check your email before bed. Ever. Long-term sleep challenges are a good conversation to have with your physician.
Can you leave your work at the office, or at the kitchen table, at the end of the day?	This one is hard, but consider leaving your laptop at the office and turning the email feature on your phone off at a certain point in the evening. Let your team know about your boundaries. If you work from home, designate a place to stash your notes and computer at the end of the day so they aren't in front of you when you're making time for yourself, for your partner or for your family.

Are you setting other interests and activities aside – including exercise – because you feel you must work more?	Make commitments to yourself and to others. Sign up for a class and prepay – that way you'll feel more compelled to go. Agree with friends and family that they can hold you to your commitments.
Do you feel compelled to always be available to everyone?	Check your ego at the door. Folks will live without you for a while. Really. Be clear about roles and boundaries with colleagues and your boss. Share the burden if someone must be available for media, or in an emergency, with others.
Are you experiencing physical symptoms of stress or anxiety – sleeplessness, stomach or digestive ailments, headaches, fatigue?	See your doctor. Listen to your body. It's a hell of a lot smarter than you are. Our gut, for example, has millions of nerve cells that work like outposts to our brain, sending it signals about our well-being. "Listening to your gut" isn't just a catchy phrase.

Are you experiencing mental and emotional symptoms of stress – short-tempered; often frustrated or angry; unable to remember important dates, names or events; and incapable of finding creative solutions to simple problems?	This is danger zone stuff and must be taken seriously. See your doctor. Stress can impact your short-term memory in significant ways. These emotional signs can indicate a decline in mental heath that can lead to serious issues like depression and anxiety.
Have you noticed – or have others noticed – a decline in your ability to maintain positive relationships with friends, family, co-workers and colleagues? If you're not sure this applies to you, ask.	For me, this is one of the most serious indicators of burnout. Constantly being frustrated with friends for asking you to do something fun, or being aggravated by colleagues when you don't share their opinion or approach, is a danger sign. Relationships are how we get things done in the social-profit world, and little else is important. Focus on this.

Have you been considering some form of self-harm, including suicide?	If you are considering hurting yourself, or are thinking about committing suicide, you *must* take this seriously. To say, "everybody thinks about these things some days" ignores the danger that depression and anxiety can have. Contact your physician immediately, and if you are thinking about suicide, contact the suicide prevention hotline in your area or visit a hospital without delay.

ENLISTING HELP

That's a lot to keep an eye out for all on your own. Consider a few ideas that might help you look for and recognize the early warning signs that your boat is taking on water.

1. Co-coach with someone who is not your supervisor. Find someone in your organization you don't report to, and who doesn't report to you, or from a similar field of work, who you can co-coach with. Set up a one-hour call or meeting once a month to help each other with efforts to work in a way that is healthy and sustainable.

2. Create a personal board of directors. This idea is from Jim Collins's book, *Good to Great*, one of my favourite volumes on management.[26] Can you find five or six people who can get together in person or by phone on a quarterly basis to

review your progress toward your personal and professional goals, and ask you the hard questions you need to address regarding your own sustainability?

3. Make an agreement with your supervisor that you will review personal sustainability goals and progress without concern for retribution or judgment. These goals – such as daily exercise or taking all of your vacation time and then some – could be outside your work plan so they aren't something you're evaluated on but help you to remain accountable nonetheless.

WHEN TO THROW THE HIGH BRACE, AND WHEN TO EDDY OUT

Finally, what should you do if you feel yourself slipping dangerously toward burnout?

1. Talk to your supervisor. Be sure you understand the organization's policy on how it supports the well-being of its team. Ask for support from your boss to help you bring your work and life balance back into alignment. Make a plan and ask for help sticking to it.

2. Learn to say "no." You won't get reprimanded or fired for creating clear boundaries that align with your work plan. If there are repercussions for an honest effort to set limits, then this is clearly not the workplace for you.

3. Ask for a leave of absence. Some enlightened organizations allow for a three-month leave of absence once every five, six or seven years

of service to allow dedicated staff to eddy out with the full support of the team. I'll dip into this later.

4. Double down on seeking support and guidance from your coach, personal board of directors or family. This is not a time to go it alone.

5. Finally, if you're at risk of suffering a major set-back due to work-related stress, starting scouting for a place to eddy out.

Notes on Technique:
The High Brace

1. When you're paddling heavy water, keep a few things in mind: The more water you take into the boat, the less maneuverable it will be. Stop often to bail. If you're running a set of rapids, keep your paddle in the water. Momentum is your ally. Don't grab the gunnels – the sides of the canoe – as this will make the boat less stable, and it means you're not paddling. Communicate with your bow or stern paddler.

2. Make a commitment to yourself and others in your life that you will do your work in a way that allows you to stay healthy and happy. Martyrdom is not productive.

3. Learn to watch for signs of anxiety, stress and impending burnout. Help one another.

4. Make a plan, review it often and find someone who can hold you accountable.

5. If you're taking on too much water, and can't bail yourself out fast enough, get help.

6. Don't be afraid to look for a quiet eddy.

Chapter 3

When to Eddy Out

What do I mean by eddy out? It means to take a break. When you eddy out, you're proactive in looking for a place to get out of the madcap, white-water rush you've been on and rest and recharge for a few days, a few weeks or a few months.

Central to this, and to be discussed in Chapter 9 about organizational support for resilience in the nonprofit workplace, is that you have the option of stepping away from your work and then returning if you want to. If this option doesn't exist through a formal leave of absence policy, through a sick leave provision in your contract or through the regulatory environment in which you work, then eddying out may well involve resigning. Before we get to that, let's consider how you will know it's time to cut the eddy fence.

Let's also assume that you have a choice. You haven't been dismissed, but you can feel yourself flailing, and despite your best efforts to brace, to bail and to get help to do so, you're taking on too much water. How do you know it's time to cut the eddy fence and take a break in quieter waters?

There is a concept in psychology called the "sunk cost fallacy," and it means pretty much what it sounds like. "I've spent three years on this campaign? How could I leave now?" was a phrase that often crossed my mind in the final few months of my time at Y2Y. My internal dialog sounded something like this: "After everything I've done? After all I've sacrificed, it seems a shame to turn my back on it now."

"Of course," says Peg Streep in *Psychology Today*, "this isn't rational thinking...[If] going to work fills you with dread, staying even longer won't help you cope with the time you now consider wasted or lost. But people do it anyway, all the time."[27] You've likely heard the phrase, "throwing good money after bad." It means that investing more money into a losing proposition isn't going to make it better. In this case, using the argument that you've already invested *all this time* and so you might as well stick it out is "throwing good *time* after bad."

You can't get time back. The time you've invested in a job that is no longer working for you is behind you now. The time you are considering continuing to invest, however, is in front of you.

Another phrase from popular psychology is "intermittent reinforcement." First coined by B.F. Skinner, a Harvard-based behavioural sociologist and psychologist, it refers to a condition where the subject responds to occasional positive rewards the same way they would to continuous positive rewards. Dr. Skinner did his research on rats, which, despite not being rewarded each time they pressed a lever for food, tried even harder.

According to Peg Streep, we're not that different from rats in this way.[28] We might know that things are pretty terrible at work, or we might be so burnt out that we can no longer cope, but from time to time we get a reward, and that makes us try even harder.

From my own experience, there are some clear indicators when it's time to leave. It's important to be highly critical of your own perception of these markers. It helps to have a close friend, partner, coach or personal board of directors available to hold you to account and insist on reflective consideration on these matters. Sometimes, when we are facing short-term challenges, we may feel any or all of these, but that doesn't mean at the first onset of anxiety we should bail out of the boat. These are perfect times to eddy out.

These indicators should be observed for their frequency and duration. A good sign that you're in trouble is if you experience these things over and over again, with increasing frequency, and have a harder and harder time recovering from them. If that's the case, you may need to start scanning the shore for a place to rest.

LOOKING FOR FLAT WATER

Here's a partial list that you might add to, and the corollary that we might strive for, during our time working to save the world, or once we've made the decision to cut the eddy fence.

If you feel this over a prolonged period of time, you may need to eddy out:	What you might strive for while undertaking your cause-related efforts, or after you take time away:
a feeling of dread at the idea of going to work;	anticipation and excitement at the work you get to do;
fear and an inability to overcome it;	joy, and the sense that this is your default emotion;
anxiety and/or chronic depression;	peace, and a feeling of ease in the world;
demoralization or feeling undervalued or unappreciated;	a feeling of being valued for your contribution;
physical health challenges;	well-being, vitality and being energized;
failing relationships;	thriving relationships;
feeling as though you have no choice.	the knowledge that you always have a choice.
What do you feel?	*What do you want to feel?*

Most of these are pretty straightforward but gallingly entwined. None of us should expect to feel energized by our work or our volunteer efforts all the time, just as nobody should expect joy, peace or a feeling of ease to be present at every moment of every day. That's not realistic. The key here is to assess what your default feeling is. If day after day you drag yourself out of bed, feeling a sense of dread that you have to go to work, or if you're constantly feeling demoralized once there, then you need to do something to change that default setting.

Feeling demoralized may lead to anxiety or depression. Failing relationships, with a spouse, your family or friends, can lead to mental or physical health challenges. If you go to bed at night with a knot in your stomach because the thought of going to work the next day makes you feel ill, or if you can't sleep, or when you do you're plagued by nightmares, you need to pay attention to those signals. If you wake in the morning and don't want to get out of bed and face the day at the office, that's a pretty strong signal. We all have days like this, but if this is commonplace for you, says Jacquelyn Smith, in *Forbes* magazine, you should probably consider cutting the eddy fence.[29]

In the "Notes on Technique" for Chapter 1, I asked, "Do you already know that it's time to eddy out?" In his book *When to Jump*, author and coach Mike Lewis explores this question in detail. He urges us to "listen to our little voice." In examples from a dozen different writers, he explores this topic in some depth.[30]

Fear will keep you from acknowledging what you almost certainly already know. This is a theme that I've noted in reading dozens of articles on the topic of when to quit a job. We can see the writing on the wall, but sometimes it's in a different language that we must first learn before we can understand it. Our guts are telling us something, but we're too afraid to listen. We're comfortable, or at least *familiar* with our situation, even if it's difficult or painful at times. We are accustomed to that pain, and even rely on it to an extent to help us create the story of who we are and why we do what we're doing. We brag about it. "Oh, I'm so busy right now. It's just crazy," we tell each other in a strange competition to see who is carrying the most stress and fatigue. In a perverse way, we celebrate each other's stress.

We can be looking straight at the sweeper – a log just below the surface of the water – but we don't see it. We have to take time to read the river; to decipher what our "little voice" is telling us. We need to eddy out.

SOLO OR TANDEM PADDLING

You don't have to paddle these heavy waters alone. As noted previously, find someone – an individual, a coach, colleague, mentor, friend, life partner or a small informal group – who can help you maintain perspective. "You never actually jump alone," writes Laura McKowen in her essay in *When to Jump.*[31]

My wife has been my greatest support. Even though it would mean a prolonged period of economic uncertainty, she encouraged – no, *strongly* encouraged – me to cut the eddy fence. It's important to have someone in your boat who isn't afraid to call you on your BS. Supporters like David

Thomson, my long-time, on-again, off-again coach and mentor at Training Resources for the Environmental Community (TREC), and Ed Whittingham, former executive director at the Pembina Institute and Friday-beer-drinking buddy, offered cool-headed, honest and sage advice.

Then there's a moment when you know. It may be deeply uncomfortable. You'll want to tamp it down and deny it. Don't. As someone who has dabbled in meditation for most of my life, I'm familiar with these moments when the discomfort in our mind permeates our entire being. When meditating, we're counselled to breathe into this discomfort, to "invite it in for tea," to embrace it, learn what it has to teach and let it go.

Most of what makes us uncomfortable is related to the story we tell ourselves about who we are and why we are here, and what we would be if we didn't have the crusader mantle to wear. The rest is almost certainly fiction created by our fear that will never come to fruition and that is merely part of our mind's way of keeping us from cutting the eddy line. It's important to train ourselves to face the cold hard facts of our circumstances and not buy into the stories we tell ourselves about who we are, what we do and why we are doing it.

"Coping is what people do when they try to muddle through," says Seth Godin in The Dip. "They cope with a bad job or a difficult task. The problem with coping is that it never leads to exceptional performance. Mediocre work is rarely because of lack of talent…. All coping does is waste your time and misdirect your energy. If the best you can do is cope you are better off quitting. Quitting is better than coping because quitting frees you up to excel at something else."[32]

Godin offers one possibility, and in the end, it may be the correct course of action for you. Quitting is one option we'll explore, but it shouldn't be your first option. What's important, however, is to explore both your decisions and your motivation. Can you take a break? Do you have some banked overtime saved up? Often we find ourselves beginning to burn out, but we haven't considered the most basic of ways to revitalize our efforts: take our vacation time.

But sometimes that isn't enough.

"Pride keeps people in careers," says Godin, "years after it's become unattractive and no fun.... Are you too proud to quit? One of the reasons people feel really good after they quit a dead-end project is that they discover that hurting one's pride is not fatal. You work up the courage to quit, bracing yourself for the sound of your ego being ripped to shreds, and then everything is okay. If pride is the only thing keeping you from quitting...you're likely wasting an enormous amount of time and money defending something that will heal pretty quickly."[33]

Godin's book is a fabulous and blessedly short read or listen for anybody looking for guidance on whether or not to quit. (That said, I could save you a few bucks and say that, if you're buying a book about deciding if you should quit, you've likely already made up your mind.) I'm giving you another possibility to consider.

In the end, a lot of people can give you advice, a few people can provide you with guidance, but only one person can really understand what you need to be happy and live a fulfilling life: you. "The question I've come back to again and again in my life is, 'What would I do if I wasn't afraid?'" Sheryl Sandberg said in *When to Jump*.[34]

What would I do? I'd cut the eddy fence.

OPTIONS WHEN CUTTING THE EDDY FENCE

Most of us have a few options available to us when it comes to cutting the eddy fence. This isn't an all-or-nothing experience. If you've gone through the process of self-evaluation, talked it over with a coach, a friend or partner, and have come to the conclusion that staying on your current course will lead to burnout, and its consequences, then it's time to explore your options.

The first one is obvious: *take your vacation*. A large percentage of the workforce in North America reports that even with just two weeks of vacation a year, many people don't take that small period of time off to rest and recuperate. Do it. If you've got some vacation time owing to you, arrange to take it as soon as possible. Consider this a mini-eddy turn, where you can rest and be still and reflect. Don't plan a trip to Europe or undertake a major house renovation during this time. Allow yourself some time to calmly reflect on your situation and evaluate your longer-term options.

Maybe a short vacation isn't going to do it, or maybe during your time off you've decided you need more time to cut through the uncertainty that often accompanies such stressful situations.

The second option available is to *ask for additional support*. This may involve working with your supervisor, your board of directors or board-staff liaison, or another member of your team, with an external support person or a professional counsellor, to gain tools and insight into how to manage the strain of your work. As noted above, this is where you'll want to be specific and rigorous in your effort to manage your symptoms of burnout, overwork and fatigue. Make a plan and work with your support person to stick to it.

If a vacation and support aren't helping, your next step is to prolong your time away from your work to re-evaluate. If your organization has a formal (or informal) leave-of-absence or sabbatical policy, explore this with your supervisor. These options often must be approved by the boss, or even your board of directors, and require some notice, so don't delay if you feel yourself taking on too much water. *Taking a leave or a two- or three-month sabbatical* may be all the rest time you need to feel prepared to re-enter the current and feel more balanced and ready for the big waves ahead.

Be forewarned that, sometimes, despite it being in an organization's best interests to keep its staff healthy and productive, sabbaticals or leaves can be denied. This could be the result of leadership that isn't aware of the dire circumstances that lead to burnout, or could be the result of difficult staffing situations that don't allow for team members to be out of the organization for prolonged periods of time. If you are denied a leave or sabbatical, explore other options, but keep in mind that only *you* can keep your own best interests in mind over those of your organization.

If your organization doesn't have a leave policy, or if you've been turned down, *explore a physician-directed sick leave.* This is a more serious step to take, and your doctor will almost certainly insist that if your emotional and mental state require this action that you should also be seeing a mental health professional. Do this too. Professional support for your mental health is vital during any time spent on shore after cutting the eddy fence.

Your final step will be to *submit your resignation.*

Notes on Technique:
When to Eddy Out

1. When you're tired, when you need to rest, when you need to scope downriver for the next obstacle or challenge, that's when finding a place to eddy out of the river is needed.

2. Previous investments of time and energy are not lost when you are considering an eddy turn; they are merely the prequel to the next reach of the river you will run.

3. Consider how you want your life to feel (peaceful, effortless, at ease?), and consider how you are feeling when you are locked in a dilemma about what to do next.

4. Pay attention to gut feelings – this is your body's way of communicating with your brain so that it has to listen.

5. Consider: How would I manage this situation if I had proper support from my organization? Can I lead my organization's efforts from within?

6. You can cut an eddy line alone, but it's easier if you have someone else in the boat with you.

7. Ask yourself, as Sheryl Sandberg has, "What would I do if I wasn't afraid?" Then do it.

Chapter 4

How to Cut the Eddy Fence

If you've exhausted your options and have made the decision that it's time to leave your volunteer position or your job, then it's time to formulate a plan for your success.[35] Consider doing this on your home computer, not your work machine. Enlist the help of your coach, your personal board of directors, a close friend or your partner.

While preparing to quit leaves you with more options, knowing you are going to get fired can afford you many of the same opportunities. Regardless of your circumstances, knowing how to cut the eddy fence is important to your long-term prospects.

As soon as you get a sense that you're going to make a change, or that a change is going to be imposed on you, start preparation for it. That includes, first and foremost, financial planning. If you have a budget, now is the time to cut all unnecessary spending. Start packing away as much money as you can so that once you cut the eddy line, you can rest there for a little while without the pressure of having to make an income. Most financial advisors recommend at least a three-month buffer, but four, five or six is much more comfortable.

In fact, start planning now, no matter what. An emergency fund of three months' bare bones expenses will reduce both the real and perceived risk when it comes time to make a transition. My wife is a superb financial planner and insisted that we create this buffer in our finances years ago, and we've maintained it ever since. (Note: Emergencies don't include beer, meals in cowboy bars in southern Alberta or camera equipment, as has been pointed out to me on several occasions.)

When you're setting these plans in place, go slow, wade in. "Jumping," as Mike Lewis says, means you're not necessarily jumping into the deep end. You can jump into the shallow end of the pool too.[36]

When directing staff, I believed that once a teammate was considering a move, it was almost certainly too late to change their mind. These ideas tend to percolate for a long time before they boil to the surface. It's likely that, if you're thinking about eddying out, part of you is already committed, and maybe a little anxious to get on with it.

This also works in reverse; if you're thinking about launching your canoe into these troubled waters, go slow. If you're considering joining the NGO world, take your time; it's not going anywhere. There is little risk that all of the world's problems will be solved as you take your time to consider nosing your boat into this particular river (but if they were, wouldn't that be nice?). This kind of work isn't for everyone. The social-profit world is very different from managing a for-profit business or working in a government agency. The financial model is different, and the lack of structure often disorientates workers entering the NGO sector from business or public service. Sit on a board of directors or volunteer for a NGO before committing to running that river.[37]

Other elements of your plan may include:

- Timing: When is the best time to leave? You may wish to stay for a few months to save more money, to finish some important work or ensure your teammates have the support they need during your transition. Remember that you are the only person in the equation who is responsible for your best interests, so ensure they are considered when evaluating timing. Other timing considerations may include using up your vacation time before resigning, and if your organization has a RRSP (501K) program, timing your departure to maximize the matching portion of the program.

- Notification: If you have the option, don't burn any bridges on the way out the door. When you hand your notice to your supervisor (and do this in person, not by email, or text, or on Snapchat), discuss with them the best timing for your departure. Do they want you to remain on the job until a replacement is found? If so, set a timeline for this. Do not leave this option open-ended. Our brains and nervous systems like to have a definite window when we know we can complete our eddy turn.

- Legal Advice: If you have any doubts about your legal standing, or if you're on probation or at risk of termination, seek professional legal advice. It's a sound investment that will help reduce the risk of backlash from your former employer and ensure you take advantage of all your legal rights.

- Logistics: Maybe you've been with your employer long enough that you have an office full of stuff. Make sure that in your planning for your departure you consider how you'll clear out your office, and do it in a way that has as little impact on your fellow employees or volunteers as possible.

- Family Life: Immediately after leaving your employment is a good time to plan for time with loved ones, friends, family and others you are close with. You'll need the support, and in the heady days after leaving a position that was burning you out, you may oscillate between being excited and disappointed. Having love and support at this time will be important.

There are other considerations as you make your plans to eddy out. You're almost certainly bound by a contract that prevents what intellectual property you're allowed to keep when you leave your job. Follow it to the letter. Don't mess this up, as it will come back to haunt you. That said, make sure that any personal contacts you have are backed up, and that information that you have generated during your employ that is not subject to your contractual agreements is available to you.

If you can, avoid burning bridges. Maybe you

need a break, or a change, or a rest; it doesn't mean you'll never come back. The social-profit world is really very small, and your reputation is the most important piece of collateral you own.

Fear is natural. It keeps us from making mistakes, but it can also keep us from making changes that are necessary. Working with friends, a personal board of directors, a coach, a mentor, a spouse or a relative can help you sort out when fear is helpful or harmful.

Be careful during this period of transition that fear doesn't manifest as anger, ego or impatience. Fear, in my opinion, is the root of anger. When we're stepping away from something that might be very uncomfortable at times, it's still familiar, and it's bound to create some additional anxiety. Keep a close check on how that fear shows up in your life.

DEALING WITH ANGER

Part of what has led to my own burnout on several occasions has been my anger. Without delving too deeply into this – something I undertook in *Running Toward Stillness* in more detail – anger and its root cause, fear, have plagued my work since I started in the environmental community more than 30 years ago.

Some of this anger may have pre-existed the dawning of my environmental consciousness – likely a result of a troubling adolescence – but I can trace this anger to my junior year in high school, when the woods I so often took salvation in were slated to be felled to make way for a toll highway, and when I started reading about issues like acid rain, the hole in the ozone layer and the greenhouse effect.[38]

How could I not be angry? As a 16-year-old, I was just beginning to articulate how important nature was to my sense of well-being and now I was learning that the whole thing was going to hell in a handbasket! As someone predisposed to ire, this emerging knowledge was like dumping fuel on a fire.[39]

Another important reference on this matter is the fabulous book by Frances Westley, Brenda Zimmerman and Michael Quinn Patton called *Getting to Maybe: How the World Is Changed.*[40] In a chapter called "Powerful Strangers," where they dissect the NGO sector's struggle with power and adversaries, the authors state, "For others who start not from safety but from rage, rebellion and a deep sense of injustice, the need is often to find forgiveness, for others and ourselves."[41]

I'm not sure if that resonates for you, but it certainly does for me. Rage, rebellion and injustice were certainly part of my motivation right through my 20s and into my 30s. As I stated in *Carry Tiger to Mountain*, however, it's not possible to remain on fire forever.[42] The fuel burns out and what is left is less than what it could be – a staggering loss of human potential and the defeat of someone who might change the world.

Cooling the flames of anger requires insight into its source, and dedication to quenching the flames. Anger is addictive because it's much more comfortable than fear, and when we're angry we can externalize our strife and assign its cause elsewhere. "Of course, I'm angry! Can't you see how messed up the world is?"

In *Carry Tiger to Mountain*, I explored the ancient Taoist philosophy of transforming anger and fear into love and compassion, and that advice rings true for me to this day. How do we do that?

1. Meditation, yoga or tai chi: Sooner or later, if you're feeling a lot of anger and fear, you're going to need a practice to transform it into something more productive. Through sitting or walking meditation, yoga or tai chi, we can direct our own energy to begin this process. It will take some time, and at first will be deeply uncomfortable, but it's worth exploring.

2. Part of what meditation does is to create the capacity for a pause so that when we feel anger arising, we can intervene. Rather than acting on our anger – lashing out at a colleague or yelling at a loved one – we can create a small space where we breathe, calm down and change that moment into a productive response (which includes, more often than not, no response).

3. Compassion is the ability to feel how others feel and to reflect on that insight for the betterment of ourselves, as well as those around us. As I noted above, we might be angry with a decision maker who has failed to provide funding to address homelessness, or a developer who is destroying endangered species habitat. We're afraid of how that will impact vulnerable populations, or that it will leave little wildness for our children to revel in. Compassion is needed

so we don't hate the person but instead can find useful solutions. Those we oppose are people too, and while we may disagree with them, even vehemently, we must remember at our core our shared humanity and create compassion as a means for finding resolutions.

4. It's likely that if you're in a situation where you're burned out, have resigned or even been dismissed, you'll be angry at your former supervisor, your teammates and even your supporters. Anger and fear are often irrational; they are about stories we tell ourselves about who we are, and maybe the wrong that has been done to us. Examine these stories and over time think about how true or not they are. Do they serve you and your effort to move forward? It may take some time, but learn to feel compassion for the challenges that those you perceive have wronged you may face. It may well be that ignorance, stress and anxiety plague them as well. In the end, harbouring lasting anger will only hurt your efforts to get back on the water.

STORYTELLING

From time to time, when I'm doing a talk or a book reading, I'll explain to people that something is a "true story," and for some reason that always gets a chuckle from the audience.

The truth is, most of the stories we tell others, and ourselves, have an element of fiction to them. These small mistruths can be one of two things: 1) an honest effort to fill in the blanks of our fallible memories with details that make for a better

How to Meditate

I've mentioned meditation several times now in this manifesto. It's likely time to provide a short tutorial on what could be an entire volume itself: how to meditate. Here I'm speaking from my own half-hearted, ill-informed and likely completely wrong perspective, so it's likely worth seeking another reference, or taking an introductory class on the subject. I sit for 15 – 20 minutes in the morning and ten or so minutes each evening.

I follow a very basic form of meditation and have since 2006:

- Make yourself comfortable. I sit on a chair with my feet on the floor, or if my knees – injured in running missteps over the years – allow, with my legs crossed comfortably. I fold one hand in the other, or sometimes will gently press the fingers of one hand into the fingers of the other. If I'm stressed, I might forget and end up in a death grip, hand in hand, and have to remind myself to relax.

- Breathe. It seems like this should be obvious, but it isn't. See if you can't catch yourself holding your breath! I choose a natural rhythm, which often slows down and deepens when I'm feeling more relaxed.

- Observe your thoughts. The purpose of meditation isn't to banish thoughts, it's to observe them and practise nonattachment. All sorts of things will pop into your mind while you are sitting – shopping lists, fantasies, memories, stories – and instead of getting attached to them, acknowledge them – they are just thoughts – and gently push them aside.

story; or 2) a somewhat less honest effort to create a mythology or fable we feel is better representative of who we are and what we want to be. "Memory, it turns out, has a surprising amount in common with imagination," says Kat McGowan in *Discover* magazine. "Conjuring worlds that never existed until they were forged by our minds."[43] "Memory distortions are basic and widespread in humans, and it may be unlikely that anyone is immune," reports Erika Hayasaki in *The Atlantic* on a study published in 2013 in *The Proceedings of the National Academy of Sciences.*[44]

When it comes to figuring out how to cut the eddy fence, consider this: You're going to make up stories in your head about what is happening to you, and how you could have gotten to this point. You wanted to save the world, but instead you're in your pajamas watching cat videos at 11 a.m.

After a while it's going to be hard to know what is true and what is fable. That's just the way the human mind works, and it isn't something you need to fret about, at least not in the context of this little book.

But you need to be aware of it.

I have stories I tell others and myself about who I am and how I wish to be perceived in the world, and those stories influenced my behaviour at work, and my departure, significantly. My story as it relates to this topic goes something like this: I work hard and intelligently to make the world a better place, but despite my decades of effort and my well-acknowledged deficiencies, I got fired.

It's a good story, but it's likely wrong, or at least

not entirely true. This is part of a larger narrative that dominates my own mythology of myself. In the story, I'm the flawed hero who, despite setting out on a quest to defeat some dragon, has been thwarted by the palace royalty. My guess is that the person who dismissed me, or the organization's board of directors, would see this very differently.

We have to be ruthless in our effort to debunk these stories we have about ourselves. Being aware of the stories we tell ourselves about our work, and our place in the world of social justice or environmental activism, will help in the process of eddying out. It will allow us to peel away some of the layers of myth and parable from our own lives so we can look more clearly at the truth of our situation. That is part of what we'll look at in Chapter 6 on taking responsibility for your own saga. We'll look at how myth making occurs in our journeys in that same chapter.

Take control of your personal narrative. Don't lie to yourself or to others about what you are doing and why. Instead, force the truth out of the experience. If you don't, your time sitting in quiet waters won't be worth as much as if you were on a personal mission to understand what is really happening.

BACK TO WATERTON

You may recall that in Chapter 1 I talked about how my decision to eddy out – interrupted or not – occurred while camping on the Belly River in Waterton Lakes National Park. The first thing I did after being dismissed was to drive back to Waterton Lakes. I had come back from the Canada Day long weekend on Monday night, was dismissed on Tuesday afternoon and on Wednesday headed back again.

I had bought a ticket for a fundraising event hosted by Alberta Premier Rachel Notley for the Tuesday, so I put on a suit, drove my pickup into the city and half-heartedly mingled at the event. I made some small talk with a few friends, drank some "free" beer[45] and left early, ditching my suit for a pair of faded jeans and a worn-out T-shirt before making the four-hour drive back to Waterton. I spent seven of the next ten days there shooting, hiking, camping and writing. I came home to collect my kids and a few days later we returned together to play photographer, fly-fish and eat ice cream.

I was learning how to be a human again, or maybe for the first time. I was trying to wash off, peel off, chisel off the layers of stress, worry, anxiety, fear and anger and to learn to be civil again. My family, my wife, my friends have never known me, this me, the real me.

In the evening, my boys and I sat in the dark on the banks of the Belly River, photographing the stars, leaning into each other in the warm night air. This was that all-important first stage of healing; the period when it's perfectly all right to ignore all the buzzing questions circling your head like mosquitos and just drift. "When your demon is in charge, do not try to think consciously. Drift, wait, obey," says Rudyard Kipling.[46] So I waited, drifting on the banks of the Belly River, the cloud of light that is the Milky Way itinerant overhead.

Starting on the night I got fired, and lasting through those first few weeks, I was deliriously excited. All the things I'd put off because I was bound to my job I could now do! I have a list of a couple dozen book projects that are important to me; I'd get started. There was nothing (except the middling challenge of earning a living, but I'll address that in Chapter 6) to stand in my way.

The ideas were swirling at that time, like pollen in an eddy, like stars in the firmament. I knew I had to pause long enough to know which ideas were ready. Ideas are like fruit and need to be picked when ripe.

Nor is the creative world inspired by fear or anger. It is love that inspires. In the first days of my departure, though living outdoors with my family, camera in hand, I was deeply angry at what I believed was a grave injustice. I had to learn how to harness that anger, gently change it into something more productive, and then use it to propel myself into the next phase of my life's work. That would take some time and patience. The first few weeks and months after my dismissal became a preparation for creativity and inspiration. When it struck, I wanted there to be no hesitation.

The trajectory of recuperation is anything but arrow-straight. It's a godawful mess, and when you're proceeding through it, there can be little wonder that sometimes we lose hope. Once the eddy fence has been cut, the world suddenly slows down, and you may find yourself watching from the shore as the rest of the world races past. Stay still awhile.

MATH AND NIGHTMARES

By August I had entered the nightmare phase of the recovery. For five nights in a row – four of them camped on the banks of the Belly River and one high above the Castle River on a bluff overlooking the foothills – I'd struggled through nightmares. In one dream, I was in Washington, DC, lobbying for a new protected area in the Badger-Two Medicine region of Montana. I showed up at a black-tie fundraiser in a bathrobe and, after knocking back a few drinks, was told I had to take a math test! In another dream I was teaching a math class and my former boss was judging my performance.

Clearly, my subconscious was lagging behind my conscious mind in casting my anger and fears to the refuse pile. My daytime explorations in the mountains were dragging in the wake of my subconscious dreaming.

It's also pretty clear I have some work to do overcoming my anxiety about math.

After four weeks of nearly continuous time in the mountains – something I hadn't had in more than 20 years – I was feeling a new anxiety: a lack of purpose and importance. When doing conservation work, I felt important, as if I was making a difference. Even when I felt I was spinning my wheels, I knew I was helping to make incremental progress toward conservation goals. Hiking out on the trails, rising early to shoot first light, looking for wildlife and returning home long enough to restock the beer cooler and make sure the kids got a fresh change of underwear every now and again was being overshadowed by my old nemesis, "a meaningful life."

"Tell me, what is it you plan to do with your one wild and precious life?" asks poet Mary Oliver.[47]

"The purpose of life is to matter, to have it make some difference that we lived at all," answers Leo Rosten.[48]

Where I was once at the centre of nearly every conversation about conservation in Alberta, now I was at the centre of very little at all. Nobody called, nobody texted. I was out of the loop for the first time in ages.

And I was still angry. A month in the mountains, with work in the rearview mirror, and I'd gained almost no insight into how to let it go. I kept asking myself, "What am I supposed to be doing?" I was often at a loss.

Two backpacking trips – more than I've been able to squeeze in than in any previous summer in recent memory – provided some perspective. Jenn and I spent four nights in Misty Basin in the Kananaskis, the longest we'd been out in a few years. It's not that we hadn't had the time; we just hadn't had the energy. By the end of a long week of gruelling work, the only thing we'd wanted to do was go for a short walk, work around the house and sit on our patio and drink wine and beer.

Another long walk with friends into the headwaters of McPhail Creek, and up onto the Continental Divide and the Hill of Flowers created more space in my head and in my heart. With the walking, I could feel, despite the confusion, an opening to some insight.

Having time to think, to feel, to be open to insight, is the point of cutting the eddy fence. With some careful preparation, a short break, a leave of absence or quitting can provide you with the room and time you need to evaluate where you are on the river, and how to navigate the waters ahead.

Notes on Technique:
How to Cut the Eddy Fence

1. Making a successful eddy turn requires a commitment. You have to commit to the maneuver or you may end up tipping, or being swept downstream – side to the river or backwards. Once you've identified the eddy you want to hit, the paddler in the stern will provide enough forward momentum that the boat will cross the eddy fence. On fast-moving rivers the fence could even present itself as a small rapid. The bigger the fence, the more momentum you'll need. The stern paddler angles the boat and when the nose has crossed the fence pries hard in the stern to swing the craft into the eddy. A few short strokes to clear the fence and you're in quiet waters.

2. Make a plan. Start now.

3. Create a budget that cuts costs so you can rest in the eddy longer.

4. Manage fear and anxiety during this crucial period through contact with friends, exercise, outdoor adventure, quiet contemplation and meditation.

5. Pay attention to your stories – some of them might be true.

Chapter 5

Forward Ferry

August 2018 brought heat and smoke as a re-cord-breaking number of fires burned across British Columbia, Montana and into Alberta. Our forays into Waterton Lakes and the adjacent Cas-tle Wildland took on a surreal feeling as the moun-tains became hazy blue lines shrouded in dark-ness. At sunset the world would become pink or yellow, and sitting on the banks of the Belly River we watched the day fuse almost seamlessly into the darkest night.

It was during this time that the gravity of what had happened started to sink in. I was adrift. The days when I was in the mountains, looking for wildlife or something that I could photograph that wasn't blurred by the pall of smoke stream-ing over the mountains from more than 500 fires in neighbouring BC, were good days. I was occu-pied and focused. But the days in between, when I was home attending to other matters, restocking or simply focused on my family, were more dif-ficult. Despite that, both my children mentioned how much more relaxed I was. Yet I didn't feel different. I was still anxious and frustrated, but I must have been behaving differently for them to point this out.

As long ago as I can remember, the people I've been working with – the people serious about making change – have struggled with depression, anxiety and rage. In 1991 I attended a conference for activists in a place called Sargent Camp, near Hancock, New Hampshire, and met Dr. Stuart Hill. Hill delivered what was for me a groundbreaking presentation on perception and healing. I came away from that event – just 20 years old – realizing that somehow I, too, had been infected with an anger that just kept growing.[49] I also knew there was a path to reclaiming my reactions to my emotions, something I continue to work on to this day.

What was I angry about? For what was lost, because our collective society seemed so ambivalent, and because I couldn't do more to change that. It's been easy over the years to admonish myself to transform that anger into love, compassion and empathy. But to maintain the lasting practice has been a much greater challenge.

The problem with anger, and its root cause fear, is that, while it might have a primary source, it doesn't restrict its impact to just one part of your life. It bleeds into everything. As noted above, one of the casualties of the sort of work I'd been doing for years were relationships. I can't count the number of times I've told my best friend J. that I simply couldn't take the time off to go backpacking, or, if I did, I'd look for ways to cut the trip short out of fear I would fall behind at work. My wife and children, patient as they are, had noted with concern my declining mental health.

Instead of listening, I just kept right on paddling, sometimes even harder to make up for the embarrassment I felt at having let people I love down.

The forward ferry is a technique used when trying to move sideways across a fast-moving body of water. Unlike on slow-moving water or quiet lakes, you can't turn your boat side to the river; you'll capsize and go for a swim. Instead, you turn about in the river and angle the boat 20 degrees into the ongoing water and paddle hard, digging in against the current. The canoe will hold its position in the river and glide across toward the desired shore.

While doing this, you might see some colleagues race by, mid-river, paddling like mad. When I was making for quiet waters, and after I'd landed, I would catch glimpses of my former life; the people I had mentored left mid-river and digging in hard to run a near constant set of rapids. Part of me wished I was in the boat with them, helping to steer around the boulders, and part of me was damn happy to be in these quieter waters, and wished they were here with me.

TAKING RESPONSIBILITY

In 1993 I had my first brush with burnout as a student activist in Ontario. Again, in 2005, after six years at the helm of Wildcanada.net I suffered another self-implosion. While in my youthful exuberance I was able to quickly bounce back, the 2005 episode took more time and extracted a higher toll. My first book, *Carry Tiger to Mountain*, was one result, and the prolonged depression and recovery that followed led to the events chronicled in *Running Toward Stillness*.

Hadn't I learned a thing? The truth was, I had, but sometimes – despite intellectual knowledge – those who are compelled to dedicate their lives to making a difference sacrifice themselves on the alter of ego, pride and unrealistic expectations.

As the summer of 2018 wore on, I realized I now had another shot at learning what to do when taking on heavy water. To do so, I had to take responsibility for my own part in being tossed overboard, and for how I would move forward the next time I got in a boat.

What led to this moment of reckoning in the summer of 2018? What happens to us when we burn out? And what are the consequences, not only for us but also for those around us, and to the good work we are trying to accomplish in the world?

Through my own personal experiences, I have deduced the following five reasons why we put ourselves in the position where we burn out, quit or get fired. You can almost certainly add many more from your own knowledge.

What happens when we fail to prioritize our own resilience:	What happens when we are able to overcome this resistance to our own well-being:
We have unreasonable expectations of ourselves, and what we can accomplish, or the expectations of others are misaligned with our abilities.	We prioritize reasonable expectations for ourselves. We are able to communicate these boundaries to others, and help them understand what we can accomplish together.
Our ego has created an inflated sense of self that we can't live up to, or creates conditions that put us in conflict with others.	We drive our ego; our ego doesn't drive us. A sense of self-worth and value is the natural outcome of a healthy ego.
We are harbouring unresolved historical problems from our past that manifest in our cause-related work.	Our work is a way to help us resolve historical problems.
Fear, revealed through anger, frustration and resentment, clouds our ability to make effective decisions.	Love for one another, and for the work we do, creates a feeling of peace that allows for effective decision making.
Structurally, the organizations we work for do little to address our own personal challenges but instead aggravate them through ineffective leadership.	Compassionate leadership recognizes that cause-related work can create unique challenges and proactively addresses these obstacles to effective work.

The Buddha said that all expectations lead to disappointment. When those expectations are compounded by our own unreasonable hopes of ourselves, they will almost certainly lead to failure. One thing that many of us in cause-related work have in common is the belief that the fate of the world rests on our shoulders. This may seem self-aggrandizing, but it's really just a condition of our expectations for ourselves. Few of us chose the path we are on because we wanted to just do our part and no more; we put our boats on this particular river with the expectation that we could save the world, or at least be a part of a team effort that made significant inroads.

Sometimes, however, others project expectations on us. As a leader, I'm certain my expectations of my teams have created stress in their lives. I have had staff who joined one of my teams and felt the immediate change in their stress levels. I've had high expectations of them, and that has created challenges in how they manage their stress. It's important as leaders that we recognize when our expectations are misaligned with the abilities and tolerance levels of those we are leading.

Whether we choose to cut the eddy fence, or are pushed across it, something happens as we steer our craft out of the main current and into quiet waters. There is turmoil, followed by a sometimes-unsettling stillness. In my first few weeks in those quiet waters, I wasn't able yet to look upstream or down to get a bearing on where I had been or where I might go. I wasn't ready.

Understanding what we might expect when we eddy out, and how to make the best of it, is critical to finding peace and learning from the experience. My own goal was to get my boat back in the water, but some reflection was in order first.

There are numerous reasons why we eddy out. Some of these are almost certainly external, but it's critical to take the time to reflect on the internal reasons. Why not try leading positive change in your workplace if you've found that it's toxic? You might, with practice, learn how to avoid such a workplace, and take responsibility for the internal circumstances that led you here in the first place.

Notes on Technique:
Forward Ferry

1. If you're in heavy water, the current pushing you further and further downstream, and you spot a quiet eddy on the far shore, you can use the forward ferry to move perpendicular to the current to reach that safe harbour.

2. Take responsibility: You're going to have to do this. Do it sooner rather than later.

3. Depression, anxiety and even suicidal thoughts are not uncommon, both in society and in the social-profit sector. They are mental illnesses and are both normal and manageable. While you may not be responsible for their onset, you can take responsibility for overcoming them.

4. Taking responsibility for your own well-being is critical to not just surviving but enjoying the process of saving the world.

5. What do you want your work, and your life, to feel like? Write this down. It's important.

6. What exactly did you expect from the work that you do?

Chapter 6

Thrown Overboard

While my own experience of being dismissed from my job has been part of the narrative throughout this manifesto, most of what we've addressed so far has been the consequence of overwork and burnout, and how to eddy out when we need a break from saving the world.

But what happens if you've been fired? While sometimes people are fired for cause – they steal something, they engage in inappropriate be- haviour in the workplace, they show up for a meeting with a key funder drunk[50] – maybe you saw it coming, or maybe you were caught off guard. Either way, you're out.

Now what?

As you might surmise, there are hundreds of ar- ticles and resources written on this topic. I hav- en't read them all, but I've made a fair dent, and rather than providing extensive footnoted quotes here, I'm going to do my best to summarize the best of what I've read.[51]

Labour laws are different in each jurisdiction in Canada and across the United States. In Can- ada, labour laws fall under provincial jurisdiction. There's also a difference between being fired for cause and without cause. I'm focusing on without

cause here. If you did something stupid or uneth-
ical, such as stole from your employer, harassed
your team or punched your supervisor, you're in
big trouble and I'm not here to advise on that. Get
a lawyer.

Just as when you were considering how to make
your eddy turn I advised making a plan, the same
goes for being fired. If you didn't see it coming and
have been caught off guard, with little or no time
for preparation, the most important thing to do is
remain calm. Don't make things worse for yourself by being hostile, and insist on time before you
sign anything.

If you have a few days to prepare, this short list
will give you things to consider if you're facing
termination.

While you're still at work:

1. Almost everything is negotiable, even when
   you're being terminated. Ask clarifying questions and take a lot of notes.

2. Take your time. It's important not to rush into
   anything related to your departure. If you're
   being asked to sign anything, explain that you
   want to read the material over and will sign
   and return it the following day. Then give it to
   a lawyer to read.

3. Ask to be allowed to say goodbye. It might feel
   terrible at the time, but unless you've got a poi-
   sonous relationship with the people you work
   with, they and you will appreciate the opportunity. If you are asked to depart without bidding

farewell, you can do what I did and call your team and meet them for a coffee or a beer.

4. Be polite. It's over. There's no sense in creating animosity on your way out. Remember, your reputation is your most important asset in social-profit work, and you don't want to give your employer a reason to say terrible things about you; it's a small work world.

Once you've left, here's what to do next:

1. Call your wife, husband, partner, best friend and let them know what happened and that you're going to need their support.

2. Don't panic. (Easier said than done.)

3. Call a lawyer. Depending on your jurisdiction and the terms of your contract, you may have the opportunity to negotiate for additional severance, an extension to your benefits, retraining or even a letter of recommendation. This will cost you, but the return on the investment will almost certainly be worth it. If nothing else, you'll know you did everything you could.

4. Reach out to your most important contacts to ensure they hear the news from you first. This is the first step to re-entering the workforce, or, as we'll discuss in Chapter 8, eddying back in.

5. Make a long-term plan, and double down on your budget. Now is the time to cut anything and everything that isn't essential. (Of course, I didn't do this. When I got laid off from Royal Roads, and when I got fired from Y2Y, I spent

my time travelling.) How long can you comfortably survive without work before the bills go unpaid? Figure that out and stay focused on maintaining strict control of your spending.

6. As part of this plan, figure out how to make the most of your time in the quiet waters of the eddy. What do you want to do? You've been handed the gift of a little time and space to figure this out. Take a course, go back to school, retrain for an emerging field of work and network your butt off.

As the bulk of this little manifesto may have demonstrated, this isn't necessarily going to be fun, especially if your ego and pride – like mine – are entangled with the work you do. That said, it doesn't need to be horrible. Maybe you have to find work right away, or maybe you have a little cushion that will allow you to take a month or two before you have to eddy back in.

You may not have asked for it, but you've got it: a break. What are you going to do to make the most of it?

Notes on Technique: Thrown Overboard

1. Maybe you dumped mid-river, or maybe you were eddying out and the eddy line tripped you up. Get to shore, dry off and take some time to learn from what just happened and scout downriver.

2. Did you see this coming? Whether you did or didn't, now is a good time to consider all the circumstances that led you to be in the water.

3. You have choices and some control in this situation. Choose wisely and don't rush.

4. The time for arguing is over. The time for embracing the next phase of your life is just starting.

5. That, too, is going to take time. Be kind to yourself.

Chapter 7

Reading the River

Maybe you've just executed the most precise eddy turn seen in the paddling world; maybe you're swimming for your life and have just managed to make it to shore: one way or another, you're in quiet waters. Now what?

You can rest almost indefinitely in an eddy, and even step onto the shore or a mid-river rock to scout downstream to read the river-evaluating hazards and thrill ride yet to come.

Starting in July 2018, and extending well into the fall of that year, I sat in the quiet waters of an eddy and considered the cacophony I had just left. Photography, family trips, backpacking, hiking, fishing and camping occupied most every waking moment during this time, and while on the outside I may have appeared "still," on the inside I was roiling, caught up in the resentment, anger and frustration I had felt after being fired.

Slowly, over time, and with help, I was able to see what had happened for what it really was: an opportunity to scout downriver from the safety of the shore, read the watercourse and set a path to follow through the rocks and waves.

I learned that, in the process of eddying out, stepping ashore and reading the river, there are some things we might expect to happen. Not unlike in the process of accepting loss, I have identified five key phases. These may be more or less applicable depending on what brought you to shore, and, because they are based on my own perception, you may wish to augment with your own observations. Here are my five, in the order in which they occur:

1. immediate relief;

2. bitterness or resentment;

3. FOMO (fear of missing out);

4. disappointment;

5. acceptance and renewal.

Consider these for a moment and ask, "What do I expect to happen?" Write these down and refer to them later in your journey.

Relief

The night before being dismissed, I had resigned myself to staying put, at least for a little while longer. I was waffling back and forth, based on my fear of the unknown. For a few hours I had resigned myself to shelving the book project I was working on and refocusing myself on my leadership role in the conservation movement. I vowed to keep my head down. It was a depressing thought. I'd never kept my head down in my life! After what I'd been through over the previous few months – the intimidation and humiliation – the thought of having to tough it out for a while was disheartening.

Of course, I didn't have to tough it out.

Twenty-four hours later – after being fired – I couldn't sleep. Suddenly, a whole world of possibilities opened up to me. I could write and shoot all summer, and complete the book on the Castle and Waterton on time! All the book projects I'd been sitting on but didn't have the time to work on I could begin to explore. I could spend my summer with my kids, rather than in a hotel in Edmonton, or in meetings that bore little relevance to the actual work of making the world a better place.

And I didn't have to suffer the humiliation of being told, over and over, that I wasn't good enough. (Mind you, the final time – being fired – would stick for a while...) I felt relief. Something bad had come to an end, and something good was about to start.

Bitterness or Resentment

After a couple of weeks of camping, hiking, photographing and fishing with my sons, the feeling of relief started to fade. This feeling of freedom was replaced by a sense of bitterness, and from that grew a steady resentment.

All of my professional life I've been motivated by a strong sense of justice – for the earth and its wild creatures and for its people and cultures. Despite my best efforts to see my departure as a justifiable dismissal, I just couldn't make sense of it. All the myriad reasons given for my probation simply didn't make sense to me. I felt as if I had been wronged, and it left me feeling demoralized. I knew it was very possible I simply wasn't seeing the reality of the situation. What about my response to being dismissed was based on fact, and what was based on the stories I had created to insulate myself from reality?

I asked my informal personal board of directors to give me the straight goods. The answer I got was that, while much of what I was telling them seemed to ring true, what did it matter? I was on shore, largely unscathed and contemplating the next reach of the river. Why did it matter how I got there?

That helped. I could see where some of my less desirable character traits might have led to my untimely dismissal, and how my actions and attitude would have given my boss justification to take the action she did. By scratching hard at these injuries, I would expose them and be able to start the process of both healing and revaluation. But nothing I would do would make me want that job back, so it was best not to scratch too hard.

The resentment lingered for most of the summer. I tried to shake it, and for days, and even a week at a time, I could lose myself in my new life. The times when I was engaged with the wild, enjoying the simple magic of photographing sunrise and sunset, and all the moments in between, were pure joy. But days trapped in the cab of my truck while it poured rain, or was so smoky I couldn't see across the valley, or the intermissions when I was at home, attending to more mundane but essential life issues, allowed bitterness to brew.

What came next was highly predictable. FOMO – the fear of missing out – or FOMS – the fear of missing something – are well-known emotional reactions in the world of cause activism.

I first recognized FOMS in a social setting when visiting Hollyhock on Cortes Island, BC, for the first time. It was an intense and unexpected experience in the immediate aftermath of the 9/11 attacks on New York City. Thirty of us from around North America – including several from New York City – were together to explore the potential that digital organizing had for changing the world at the inaugural Web of Change event, led by Jason Mogus. Brought together by a common passion for change, and cemented by the emotionally raw events of the previous week, we stayed up all night in cathartic revelry. Nobody wanted to miss a moment, so for three nights and four days we basked in the richness of one another's friendship. Nobody wanted to miss out.

I realized soon after that my professional life was punctuated by FOMO as well. I hated being left out of important decisions, or being absent from key events in the conservation movement's endeavours. I'd fly across the country to attend a meeting; I'd work all night to ensure that my organization or myself was represented in a decision. I wanted to be a part of what was going on, but it was more than that. I feared *not* being a part of what was going on. Missing something meant I wasn't important; missing out meant I might be left out.

Imagine, then, what happens when you get fired from a job where you're at the centre of many, if not most, major discussions and decisions in a particular field. Cabinet ministers would call or text, looking for suggestions; foundations would turn to you for advice on how to spend their money. Reporters and pundits sought your comments for print, TV, radio.

And, then, nothing. The door slams and there is silence.

Disappointment

As the summer wore on, that silence became louder. I knew the world would keep turning without me. While plagued with an exaggerated sense of self-importance, I felt confident that the campaigns I'd been leading would continue on. Why fire me if they would be at risk, I reasoned? No, what bothered me was just that: they *would* go on without me. My phone stopped ringing, my email inbox magically emptied and nobody sought my advice or counsel any more. I was missing out, and missing it.

By the end of August and into September, I was disappointed and depressed. I became anxious again after several months of feeling calmer, more sanguine. I was disappointed with my former organization, with my colleagues who seemed to just carry on without me, with the organization's leaders who didn't appear to notice my absence, but most of all I was disappointed with myself.

I let this happen. And not just the termination. What I let happen was far worse than that: I allowed myself to be consumed, once again, and without my really noticing, by the cause. I failed

to observe the patterns that led to my own burn-out, and instead of cutting the eddy fence I let the waters swamp me once more.

When I quit after six years as founding executive director of Wildcanada.net, I knew I was cooked. Everything was exploding – my relationship, my ability to raise money or be an effective leader, even my parenting of my newborn son Rio. But at Y2Y I didn't really notice it. Yes, I was depressed and anxious, but I blamed that on post-traumatic stress from my mother's death and my reaction to that. Yes, I had been on medication for almost two years, but, again, I chalked that up to the trauma of having been with my mother while she suffered a terrible death from cancer.

I didn't see – despite my friends, my wife and even my children telling me – that the job was taking its toll. I didn't see it because I didn't want to see it. I both loved and hated the work, much in the way an alcoholic loves and hates the next drink. I had allowed the work to define me and, as a result, couldn't imagine what it would be like to lose the meaning it brought me. I was dependent on it for my sense of self-worth.

Hadn't I seen this exact same thing just a dozen years before when I left Wildcanada.net in a slow-motion disaster? I wrote my first book, *Carry Tiger to Mountain*, while the ashes of that self-immolation still smoldered around me.

As summer passed into autumn, I felt the encumbrance of my self-disappointment weigh down my progress. There isn't much that is more pitiful than a person in the grip of self-loathing.

There have been times through this process when I've hated myself, for what I'd done, what I'd become and what I'd let happen. But for the strength and counsel of good friends, a fine therapist, my loving wife and insightful children, I might have lingered there longer.

Acceptance and Renewal

Acceptance is not surrender; acceptance is a strategic decision that recognizes the reality of whatever situation you are in, evaluates the best options for advancement and leads to the next risk as we move forward.

For me, acceptance came late in the autumn of 2018, after about six weeks of long days spent editing photos from the summer, a few weeks of mapping out my next book projects and a renewal of my purpose in the world of change advocacy.

It was risky as hell.

This is the moment when we point the nose of our craft back into the current and commit to rejoining the flow. Our boat may be unstable as it cuts the eddy fence once more and the water simultaneously pushes on one side and pulls on the other. The craft comes about swiftly – the higher and harder the current the faster the turn – and then we're in it again.

The acceptance that led to the decision to make the eddy turn was at once pragmatic and idealistic. After five months of chasing the light across southwestern Alberta, I had to start earning some money to keep my family afloat. I also knew that just recording the world through the lens and with

my pencil wasn't going to be enough. I was still driven by a powerful urge to make a difference.

My renewal, however, had to be approached with caution. Five months may seem like a lovely stretch of time to lounge next to rivers while your kids fish, or hike mountain trails looking for wildlife or wildflowers, but in reality it is still a pretty short period of time.

Was I ready? Had I learned what I needed to?

It was time to put that to the test.

WHAT I READ IN THE RIVER

Five months of being shore-bound, reading the river and formulating my intention for how to rejoin the flow came down to three things:

1. What was in my personal power to change? Where was I personally incompatible with the activism-driven life I had chosen and what could I do about it?

2. What structural changes might cause-based organizations make in order to better serve their missions and mandates?

3. What new styles and forms of leadership are required in order to support both the people and organizations needed to make the world a better place?

There are a million books, articles and cheesy posters that express the simple idea that there are things within our power to change and things outside our power to change. Learning to distinguish between these is important to our mental health, as well as our success in navigating the rivers we journey on.

Stories play a vital role in our culture and in our society. Stories are the foundation of how we relate to one another and the world around us. We create our world through stories. We are all storytellers. We tell ourselves stories about who we are, where we come from and where we are going. We define ourselves through these stories, the basis of them often partially or completely fictitious.

Our own stories are deeply influenced by the archetypal stories that have been part of human culture for thousands of years. In the save-the-world business, it shouldn't come as a surprise that the archetype of the hero plays heavily to our cause-based lives. We are on a quest (one of seven archetypal stories) to defeat a monster (another of the archetypes). In our quest, we band together with others to create organizations that work much in the way a company of adventurers struggles together to tackle some great wrongdoing. The monster we are trying to defeat is not mere allegory; it is climate change, it is poverty, it is inequality and justice. It doesn't take much inquiry to see that the real monster in need of defeating is us. It's ourselves, the whole of society, and that inevitably creates a tricky conflict to navigate.

"The hero's main feat is to overcome the monster of darkness: it is the long-hoped-for and expected triumph of consciousness over the unconscious," says Carl Jung in *Archetypes and the Collective Unconscious.*[52] That is the way it's supposed to work, at least. The conclusion to the story is that the hero – us – along with our company of adventurers – our fellow volunteers, employees and supporters – slay the monster – climate change – and ascend to the throne of victory.

Sounds good, doesn't it? The problem is, it's obfuscation.

"Every hero has a shadow," says Scott Jeffrey.[53] Our shadow is our "dark" side, the balancing equation to our story about ourselves as a hero trying to save the world. It might be rooted in any number of things, not the least of which is childhood trauma, expectations of ourselves and others and the need to fulfill our deepest, most unconscious desires for self-actualization and meaning.

Our shadows are inevitable; they are a product of standing in the light, and that's something we can almost certainly not avoid in our efforts to make the world a better place. Just as they are inevitable, so, too, they must be confronted and embraced in order for us to live truly fulfilling lives.

"The Hero's downfall is that he doesn't know and is unable to acknowledge his own limitations. A boy or a man under the power of the Shadow Hero cannot really realize that he is a mortal being," say Moore and Gillette. "Denial of death – the ultimate limitation on human life – is his specialty…. When we do not face our true limitations, we are inflated, and sooner or later our inflation will be called to account."[54]

We think the hero must be infallible, but, of course, none of us are. Every hero from mythology has a fatal flaw, and so do we. It might be ego, it might be hubris or nearsightedness when seeing the challenges of the world, but our flaws and how we perceive them are what define us.

"The 'death' of the Hero in the life of a boy (or a man) really means that he has finally encountered his limitations. He has met the enemy, and the enemy is himself. He has met his own dark side, his very unheroic side," say Moore and Gillette. "With the death of the Hero archetype comes the emergence of true humility. And this humility only comes when we learn our limitations," adds Jeffrey.[55]

And so, through trial and error – being thrown out of the boat, capsizing, taking on heavy water, helping with a few mid-river rescues and ultimately finding a quiet place to eddy out – we come to be the true hero of the myth. Deeply flawed but self-aware, passionate and determined but humble about what we can do and how we must care for others and ourselves in the effort.

All of this is to say that, in the save-the-world business, it's hard not to see ourselves as the hero on a quest to defeat the monster of injustice or global climate calamity. The trouble is that we don't fully understand the role the hero plays in our story. The hero isn't there to defeat the monster, rescue the princess or return with the elixir of life; she or he is there to confront the shadows within themselves and, in doing so, mature to adulthood from the adolescent described by Moore and Gillette and others.

If you're wondering what this has to do with taking a break from saving the world, it is this:

when you eddy out, it's a good time to contemplate this shadow that follows us around. You can ignore it and opt to paddle another reach of wild river, but there's a pretty good chance that if you do, you're going to be swimming some heavy water once more.

When you cut the eddy fence you can step out of the boat and scout downriver. This is the time to reconcile yourself with your own personal narrative, to confront and hopefully address some of these monsters. You don't need to do this all at once; it's a lifetime's work. You must, however, be ruthlessly honest with yourself. Don't get back into the boat until you have been.

Notes on Technique:
Reading the River

1. Take a moment and walk downstream. Find a place where you can see what's around the next bend in the river. Do you see those rocks just beneath the surface? Hit those broadside and you're going into the drink. But look, that tongue of water, how smoothly it splits the big boulders and leads to a set of rolling waves – that will be a fine piece of water to paddle. Take it all in.

2. What stories are you telling yourself and others about who you are and what you're here to do?

3. Can you recreate that story so it serves you and the world around you in a healthy way?

4. As you journey through the five phases of acceptance, what are you learning that you can apply to the next stage of your work?

5. What is in your personal power to change? What can you lead?

6. How is your personal narrative incompatible with the activism-driven life you have chosen, and what can you do about it?

Chapter 8

Bow-In and Pointing Downstream

From my time reading the river, I knew how I wanted to make the eddy turn back into the current:

1. With compassion and love as my guiding principles.

2. Through creativity, for problem solving, addressing the wicked challenges we face and my own art forms.

3. By creating ample time and space around me to address the problems that had led me to near disaster in the first place on an ongoing basis.

4. By managing my emotions.

5. By continually seeking balance: with exercise, better relationships with friends and family, meditation, therapy and a renewed perspective of the world around me.

This would address the personal challenges that I needed to. How would I address the structural and leadership issues? By writing this little book. And so it begins, the next reach of the river.

I wrote extensively about the importance of compassion and love in *Carry Tiger to Mountain*. Much of my work over the last three decades has been the product of ire, frustration and most predominantly fear. Fear of what? Losing what I love; losing what I value and depend on for my well-being. Ironically, it is fear that fuels the anger of those I so often come into conflict with over conservation issues. While I fear losing a forest that brings me peace, and harbours wildlife and species at risk, others might fear the closing of a mill that might spell disaster for their community, or their perceived freedom to recreate where and how they want with their family and friends.

Understanding that fear underlies much of the hate, anger, misunderstanding and violence that plagues our culture, and keeps us from achieving the just, sustainable society we hope to, is part of the process of acting out of compassion. When we feel compassion for each other, it becomes possible to see new perspectives and understand motivations. When we understand what is driving the root cause of human behaviour, we can begin to find solutions that will address all perspectives on a challenge, and in so doing create durable results that won't unravel once the dust settles on a decision.

While it might seem very challenging when faced with anger, acting out of compassion rather than fear or disillusionment is vital. It is essential to find solutions but also to ensure that the people who have the capacity to do so remain healthy and whole through the process.

When you're ready to re-enter the flow, you nose the bow – the front – of your boat toward the eddy line. This is called "going bow-in." Generally, you angle the craft upstream here in order to allow the water in the main stem of the river to grab hold and swing you back cleanly into the current. Sometimes a high brace or deep draw from the bow-paddler is needed to execute this clean turn.

To engage the world bow-in – straight onto the problem – is the best way to rejoin the current and act with compassion and love. Love is the opposite of fear. Some would argue that love and hate are opposites, but hate is just an extreme expression of being afraid, and so I suggest that love is its contrasting emotion.

When we feel love for one another, even when at loggerheads over something important, we can begin to understand each other. Oftentimes that love is extremely difficult. Sometimes we have to suspend our judgment and love unconditionally, knowing it is likely to be unrequited. Solutions grow out of that ability to love without limitations. So does lasting resilience.

THE ROLE OF CREATIVITY

I have spent a great deal of my career in anger, in despair and in disbelief at what the world has come to. I've been frustrated, abhorring the people who have perpetrated what I consider to be crimes against humankind and the planet that sustains us. Put bluntly, however, this has not helped. Even what I sometimes refer to as "productive anger" – where I allow my resentment and antagonism to fuel me for a short time to inspire creativity or endurance – has not led to long-term productive solutions. Nor does it create the sense of peace needed to endure in this difficult culture of change.

Creativity is a by-product of compassion and love and is the backbone to finding solutions to the problems that vex us, and to help us eddy out and then eddy back in. There is a well of creativity we can all draw upon. Some of us express it through various forms of art, such as pottery, painting, photography or writing; others through crafts; and others still through cooking, gardening or carpentry. We all have access to this storehouse of creativity, and can choose to funnel it through ourselves to help us address the issues we confront in the social sector, as well as restore our own well-being when we need to eddy out.

Expressing my creativity through writing and photography is one of the principal ways I can ground myself and restore myself after having to eddy out. It's as if I'm stepping out of the canoe and finding a quiet place on the bankside, refilling my sense of wonder and awe before pointing my boat back downstream. That same well of creativity can be applied to complex problem solving.

Part of my regular maintenance of good health and resilience is to be in nature, with my family and friends, and most often with a camera or two. A regular practice of creativity can bolster our ability to withstand the challenges we face both internally in social-profit organizations and externally when facing a world that seems bent on its own demise. I have friends who quilt, paint, throw pots (not literally, through that might help too), sculpt, build furniture and scribble madly in notebooks as a way of remaining connected to the magic of the creative world, and as a means of staving off burnout, fatigue and stress. When we are lost in creative thought and action, we enter a meditative state and recharge ourselves as the energy of imagination courses through us.

All creativity – be it artistic or problem-solving skills – originates in the same place, so when we are harnessing our imaginations we are practising addressing other challenges as well.

EMOTIONS AND PASSIONS

My emotions often get the better of me. Some would suggest I'm overly emotional, and some say I'm passionate, but however you slice it, I'm sometimes at the whim of my feelings. Learning to exert some control over my emotions, rather than allowing them to control me, is a critical part of the next phase of my own journey.

It's not as if I haven't been trying. I have had a meditation practice for well over a decade, and this has been very helpful. Meditation helps us create a gap or a space between stimulus and response. Something happens – bad news on the grant front, or a catastrophe that impacts our work – and we react. The practice of meditation allows us to slow these responses down, and to choose how we react rather than doing so on impulse.

Failure to manage our emotions can lead us to a feeling of precarious imbalance. The times when I've needed to step out of the world of social change have been when I've been deeply out of balance. Fifty- or 60-hour weeks, long nights, working weekends, and forgetting to eat well, exercise and spend time in nature have been the things that most often throw me off balance. One of my great personal ironies is that, despite having dedicated my life to the conservation of nature, when I'm working hardest to protect wild places I spend the least amount of time in them.

It's easy to talk about balance, but it's much harder to achieve. Everyone has a different balance point; the right ratio of hard, thoughtful work and time away that helps ensure they remain productive and effective, both at work and in the rest of their lives. In the social-profit sector, we've been conditioned to believe that to make the world a better place we have to sacrifice ourselves to succeed. This is a form of violence perpetrated against ourselves. Thomas Merton wrote,

> There is a pervasive form of modern violence to which the idealist...most easily succumbs: activism and over-work. The rush and pressure of modern life are a form, perhaps the most common form, of its innate violence.
>
> To allow oneself to be carried away by the multitude of conflicting concerns, to surrender to too many demands, to commit oneself to too many projects, to want

to help everyone in everything is to succumb to violence.

The frenzy of the activist neutralizes his (or her) work...it destroys the fruitfulness of his (or her)...work, because it kills the root of inner wisdom which makes work fruitful.[56]

This act of self-inflicted pain may stem from a sense of grief or anger that arises from the fear and loss that accompanies much of our work. It may be rooted in feelings of powerlessness, hopelessness or frustration. Further, it may arise from unaddressed issues elsewhere in our lives that cause us to inflict this form of violence on ourselves, and consequently on others around us. "Whether you have power or you don't, chances are that you need to confront your own frantic heart – your suspicions of and anger with the other," say Westley, Zimmerman and Patton in *Getting to Maybe*.[57]

The path back to balance starts with love and compassion and the belief that our own personal resilience is inextricably linked to the long-term outcomes we want to see for the world around us. We cannot "save the world" by sacrificing ourselves.

More so, we deserve wellness.

LOW BRACE TO MAINTAIN BALANCE

Finally, on this point, resilience, wellness and personal sustainability are needed to ensure that we can enjoy the fruits of our labour, and that our communities continue to flourish after we've made the final eddy turn.

The low brace is similar to the high brace, but it's used to steady the boat in quieter water. Instead of reaching up and slapping the blade of the paddle down onto the cement-like waves of heavy water, it's more of a gentle tap to keep the boat balanced.

For me, there are five key ways to seek and maintain balance. I've never mastered any of these but continue to strive to be better and better.

1. Mental health through meditation and counselling.

2. Physical health through exercise, a healthy diet and enough sleep.

3. Emotional health through immersion in nature.

4. Relationship health through an investment in friends and family.

5. Spiritual health, however we wish to define it.

Meditation

For me, the foundation for achieving balance in my life is meditation. Wobbly at the best of times, my mental health suffers badly when I'm not paying attention to it. The most effective way I have found to do this is through a practice of daily meditation.

I'm not going to mislead you: meditation is hard work. Certainly at first it is (and, for me, that lasted for a few years...OK, maybe five or ten). The mind resists being still and empty, and rushes to fill the void with all manner of crazy thoughts, memories, fantasies, regrets, hopes, to-do lists and demands. Meditation is not the banishment of these thoughts but the acknowledgment of them and the practice of nonattachment.

Meditation comes in many forms and there are lots of great resources to help you with your practice. Some people enjoy walking meditation as taught by the Vietnamese monk Thich Nhat Hanh. Many others find yoga or tai chi practices can help achieve similar results.

The notion is to create a space in our hearts and our minds that is clean, clear and empty, which in turn can create space in our daily lives between what happens and how we respond. Meditation is the process of creating space between our response and what triggers a response so we can bring balance and peace into our lives and those around us. Meditation, when practised regularly, and for a long period of time, can provide us with insight into the true nature of the universe and our place in it. It's not for me to tell you what that might be; it's for you to discover on your own.

For the last couple of years, I've ended each of my near daily practices with a short prayer. After my timer chimes, I take a deep breath and press my hands together and say, "May my meditation, however humble, serve to bring peace and end suffering within me, within those around me and in those around the world."

Counselling

While meditation is the foundation of my mental health maintenance efforts, I'm also a proponent of mental health therapy. Where there was once more stigma around how we address our mental health, today it's not uncommon to find yourself swapping stories with friends and colleagues about your preferred form of therapy and which counselling service is best.

Understanding that you're not alone in your effort to maintain a healthy and balanced mental health regime can be liberating. Find what works for you. Over the past decade that has meant occasional visits to both my family doctor and a counsellor to work through challenges with stress, anxiety and depression. A few years ago, after a prolonged and at times dangerous bout with depression and trauma following the death of my mother, I began to take low doses of antidepressants. All combined, my physical and mental health regimen has helped restore some balance and made it possible for me to eddy back in.

Unless you believe your mind, your thoughts and your emotions exist somewhere outside your body, then it's easy to understand how mental and physical health are related. Keep me out of the gym, off my bike and off the trail for a few days and everybody around me will get the picture pretty quickly. Our physical health, how we eat, how much we exercise and how well we sleep are dominant factors in how we perform at work, interact with friends and colleagues and how we function in society.

Physical Activity

First things first: we're not all athletes. I'm certainly not. We can't all strap on our running shoes and go for a 10-k jog at lunch and be back fresh as a daisy at our desks by 12:55.

Setting that aside, nearly all of us have the opportunity to eat well and get enough sleep and enjoy some form of exercise. Serious issues with diet and sleep should be addressed by a doctor, and ensuring that exercise is done in a healthy way is a matter for a trainer, a coach or a knowledgeable friend.

I'm a proponent of daily exercise. Our bodies and minds crave habit. That said, my daily workout is one of the first casualties of being stressed, depressed or too busy. This, of course, is a vicious cycle, as lack of exercise creates the conditions for bad food choices (mmm, donuts), putting off a visit to the gym and poor sleep. These then lead to anxiety, stress and fatigue – the cycle intensifies.

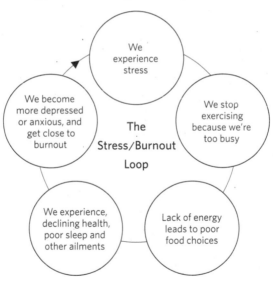

What if we could intervene in this vicious cycle? Prioritizing exercise is a good place to start. When we do this, be can begin to break the above stress/burnout loop. Imagine if, instead of sacrificing exercise, we emphasized its importance? That might help us continue to make healthy food choices, maintain better health and sleep, and armour ourselves against the impacts of stress, depression and anxiety. It's not the only solution, but it is one, and it's important.

If you're part of an organization, talk with your boss and co-workers about highlighting this. If you work in an organization that doesn't value this, or isn't able to understand the value that good health brings to the work environment, consider becoming an advocate for this. Lead by example, and encourage others to exercise with you. You can't save the world if you have an emotional breakdown or die of a heart attack.

I schedule my exercise and generally negotiate a longer lunch break to accommodate this and eating. An hour and a bit is usually enough to get to a nearby gym, go for a vigorous walk, a quick cross-country ski, run or to a yoga class, and still eat before returning to the job. I try to mix it up; one day I'll lift weights, the next ride a bike or run on an elliptical machine, and sometimes I'll climb in the indoor gym in my hometown of Canmore. Do what works for you, and start slow and build toward a fitness goal.

The rewards are nearly immediate. Within a few weeks of starting and maintaining a regular exercise regime you'll notice an increase in vitality and energy, a positive change in your appetite, better sleep patterns and lower stress.

During my conservation career, there have been a number of periods when I fell out of this routine. The pressure at work would build and I would justify skipping my lunchtime workout or walk to push through some pressing challenge. The phone wouldn't stop ringing, or I'd suffer an expectation overdose, where I would impose, or sometimes have imposed upon me, an unrealistic expectation that I simply couldn't meet in a regular eight, nine or even ten-hour day.

It doesn't take long to fall out of the habit of exercise. And when you consider starting again, the body and mind will make all kinds of excuses not to. Ignore them, and ignore the part of your ego that says, "I'm feeling soft and I can't do this today," or "How will anybody possibly function if I turn my phone off for an hour to go to a yoga class?" Trust me: they will survive, and while it might hurt both mentally and physically to keep a routine up, you're doing yourself, those around you and whatever cause you serve a great service by doing so.

Once you're exercising on a regular basis, your body will naturally start wanting healthier food to burn as fuel. When I fall out of my daily exercise routine, I default to terrible eating habits (mmm, donuts). One of the most dangerous situations is driving. During my time at Y2Y, I drove to Edmonton, or Montana, on average once a month. You pass a lot of Tim Hortons donut shops between Canmore and Edmonton.

Healthy Diet

This is one area where I struggle. When I'm under stress, I eat like a 14-year-old boy (something I have also experienced second-hand with my own 14-year-old son). I crave empty calories and carbohydrates, none of which provide me with much needed energy or long-term resilience. I know I should be eating proteins like Greek yogurt, but instead I crave ice cream.

As noted in the "Stress/Burnout Loop" diagram above, poor food choices are part of a vicious loop that leads to lack of fitness, poor-quality sleep, depression and poor self-esteem. Intervening in that cycle can help break that negative feedback loop. Starting the day with healthy food choices - for me, fruit, homemade granola and Greek yogurt - and continuing on with healthy foods can energize my work and prime me for a late afternoon workout.

Sleep

According to many experts, we in North America are plagued by a sleep deficit disorder that borders on being dangerous.[58] While the recommended eight hours of sleep per night for an adult still remains, many of us are getting only six or seven, and some far less.

Everything we do suffers when we're not sleeping. We don't want to exercise when we're tired, and we tend to make bad food choices when fatigued. Our memory and problem-solving capacity goes down the tubes. In short, we're impaired, and we more easily lose perspective, leading to increased mental health stress.

Prioritize good sleep. Toss the phone or the tablet before heading to sleep. No, it's not more calming to watch *Game of Thrones* before nodding off. It just feels that way because we've become conditioned to crave passive entertainment in the absence of other forms of relaxation. I'm just as addicted to Netflix as the next person, but I know that if I spend too much time in front of a screen before bed, it's not good for my ability to fall asleep and to sleep well.

I try to get to sleep by 10:30 each night, and try to get up around 6 a.m. Like exercise and a healthy diet, this takes discipline and I'm not always able to hold myself to this routine. I've also learned to take short naps, especially on long drives or during particularly difficult days. For me, the optimum time is 11 minutes – no idea why – which gives me just enough time to fall asleep, rest for a moment and wake refreshed.

If we're taking care of our bodies, and we're being attentive to our minds, we can also more easily address our emotional health.

Nature

Different, but connected to our mental health, our emotional health is about finding fulfillment and joy in life. We all do this in different ways. For me, and many others, a connection with nature is important to ground my emotional well-being. It also happens that nature is a great place to exercise and find solace for our mental health. You can be in nature with friends and family, and some of us would go so far as to explain that nature is the foundation of our spiritual well-being.

But we're getting ahead of ourselves.

I'm fortunate that I live in a town that is surrounded by natural, wild places. But even if you live in a city, there are almost always natural places to visit. Simply finding a small park with some trees to lie under and watch the leaves in the breeze can connect you with the natural world.

And here is why this is important: when we experience the natural world, we are coming in contact with the fundamental truth that each and every one of us is connected through the strands and fabric of life to one another and every other thing in our magnificent, if not more than a little messed up, world.

This isn't intellectual knowledge – it's biophysical. We know this in the core of our beings. Don't think you can take an hour or two a week to relax by walking in your neighbourhood park or lying under a tree watching the leaves blow in the breeze? Just watch what happens when you don't.

Recall before in the previous chapter that we explored how each of us is connected to one another. The natural world is the most obvious place to affirm that understanding. In nature, the connection between living beings and their surroundings is palpable. By immersing ourselves in nature from time to time – I would suggest as often as every day – we can invite that understanding to be a part of our emotional health.

Relationships

This isn't a book about your marriage. In fact, I'm possibly the last person you want to take relationship advice from. That said, part of finding balance is building and maintaining healthy relationships with our friends, family and partners, so in the effort to eddy back in, we've got to address this.

A few things happen to me when I'm out of balance. First, I stop getting together with friends. Like diet and exercise, these things seem as though they can be put off to a less hectic time. "I can go a few weeks, or even a month, without seeing friends. I just need to get through this bit of work and then I'll have time for them," I'll reason. A week or a month can turn into two, then six and suddenly a year will go by without spending time with my closest friends.

Relationships ground us and give us foundational support for healthy lives and a return to balance. One of the first things I did after cutting the eddy fence was to go backpacking with a few friends for five days. It put things into perspective and helped me remember what was truly important in my life.

Our relationship with our family is also one of the first casualties of overwork, stress and anxiety. My children are the most important people in the world to me, and yet when I'm crushed with deadlines, it's easy to justify long hours at the office, or disappearing at night to work on emails because "I'm doing this so they will have a better world." Worse, when I'm facing pressure to complete mounting tasks, working too many hours and feeling frustrated by a lack of exercise and sleep, I'm short, grumpy and often irritable. How is that helping my family enjoy the fruits of my labour?

Isn't it amazing that many people in North America don't use their allotted vacation time? This is nearly epidemic in nonprofit organizations, where we carry forward our vacation days until we've got weeks of extra time on our hands, we're burnt out, performing poorly and not speaking with our spouses and our friends because we're in internal chaos.

This particular point links to the following chapter on how organizations can help address the issues raised in this book. Leaders in our organizations often encourage us to take our time off, sometimes going so far as creating rules about employees not being able to carry over vacation time. Then, and sometimes in the same breath, unobtainable expectations are created – budget or planning timelines are set in the middle of summer, or a staff retreat is planned during a period when we might otherwise be hoping to spend time with friends and family. One of my favourite charitable foundations – and this despite being one of the most progressive in the business – has its granting deadline on January 1 each year. The number of times my team, my wife – who has worked in development for decades – and I have been writing grant proposals over the Christmas break is disappointing.

We have an obligation to prioritize the health of our relationships while doing the work that will make the world better for us all.

Spiritual Health

We shy away from talking about our spiritual health, maybe out of fear that by doing so we would inadvertently offend someone, or maybe because, like our mental health, our spiritual well-being is taboo.

The social-profit world prides itself on a pluralistic approach – one that embraces diversity and actively seeks out tolerance. In addition to pluralism, we often espouse a desire for diversity of world views. Some sectors of civil society have accommodated these perspectives better than others, with the environmental community still lagging far behind those who work in the social justice sector.

Despite having written about the importance of spiritual health in our efforts to make the world a better place, I, too, have been hesitant to embrace it in the workplace. Too often I've seen this go horribly wrong when discussions about spirituality are confused with religion – which it is not – or given short shrift (OK, our 15-minute breakout groups on spirituality are over, it's time to move on to budgeting and HR!).

We are each responsible for our own spiritual well-being, and what that means is as diverse as there are people on the planet. Our work, as Kahlil Gibran has said, is "love made visible," and when we are at our best, love and spirit are inextricably linked.[59]

In our effort to restore ourselves to balance, let's not overlook spirituality because it's a difficult subject to address.

THIS IS NOT A HOLIDAY

If you thought that stowing the paddles in the boat and stepping out onto the shore was going to be a little vacation, by now you've realized that it's not. You're going to discover all sorts of things about yourself, about your work and the world around us that aren't going to be pleasant or easy to face. Some of these are going to be stories that you make up; some of these stories might even be true.

The truth is we've got to do this work. There are very few people who don't have to face the shadow in their own lives, and, frankly, I find it hard to trust those people in leadership roles. The real work to be done while you're on the shore, scouting downriver, is about figuring out what you want to do with your one precious life, how you can contribute to making the world better without burning yourself into a piece of spent charcoal, and, then, finally, determining how to get back on the river, if that's what you want to do.

Before we head bow-in to the current, however, there is one final chapter I'd like to share with you. While taking personal responsibility is the most important factor in our own well-being and how we do our work, we should also address the culture of the save-the-world sector, and how we might redesign it so it's more effective and well-being-focused.

Notes on Technique:
Bow-In and Pointing Downstream

1. The maneuver: the eddy turn, in reverse: we point the bow of our craft upstream to the top of the eddy, and then with a few deft strokes nudge the bow of our boat into the current once more and are swept back into the flow.

2. How do you want to make your eddy turn back onto the river? What is important to you about that?

3. Have you allowed yourself to work through the stages of grieving and acceptance? If not, you'll likely find yourself back on the shore fairly soon.

4. What can you do to prioritize your whole health – body, mind, spirit – and the health of your relationships?

5. Will you agree to committing as little violence against yourself as possible in your work to save the world?

Chapter 9

Rescue Mid-River

We need to change the save-the-world culture. While personal reflection and growth is the first and most important aspect of preserving our own wellness and resilience in the face of the challenges of working in the NGO world, there are important cultural changes needed as well.

When one of your paddling companions capsizes a boat mid-river, you can come to their aid using what's called a "canoe-over-canoe rescue" (sometimes called a "T-rescue"). When a boat is upside down in the water, an airlock forms that makes flipping it a challenge. To right the boat, you form a *T* between your boat and the overturned one, with the capsized boat's bow to your port or starboard gunnel. Then you grab the bowline, or the handle on the bow, and lift the boat over yours, releasing the airlock. Then the rescued boat is pulled so it is resting its gunnels on your boat's, you flip it over and slide it back onto the water. During this time, the rescued paddlers hold onto the bow and stern of your boat. Don't let them upend your canoe, thrashing around trying to get in. Once their boat is back in the water, you can steady it and they can climb in more easily.

Here a mid-river rescue is analogous to what is needed to help nonprofit organizations be effective; some have capsized and their paddlers are in trouble.

CREATING A CULTURE OF RESILIENCE

Organizations spend time – some more than others – in schooling their staff and volunteers about the threat of burnout and the need to armour themselves against it.

There is a practical element to maintaining staff: hiring and training staff is timely and costly, and so maintaining an effective staff complement is in the best interest of an organization. There is also the added benefit that healthy, happy team members will function more effectively and accomplish more toward their goals. That said, there are important structural changes needed across the social-change sector that will make it possible for leaders to maintain their momentum and remain effective in guiding organizations toward success.

It's possible that, due to my own experiences in the nonprofit sector over the last 30 years, I am misreading the situation. Maybe the culture of the save-the-world movement is as healthy or healthier than any other work environment. The two questions I always ask myself when pressed to defend my views on these matters are: 1) Are we winning? If what we're doing is working, then we'd be winning more battles, right? and 2) Are we happy doing it? If we're happy doing it, then turnover would be low, morale would be high and levels of employee burnout would be negligible. My take is that we can work to improve our workplace culture in order to support teams and individuals to do good work, while ensuring they live happy, fulfilling lives.

This is a challenge that has a clear solution, something that may appeal to nonprofit activists who often face complex, Gordian-knot-like problems with no clear answers. What is required to address burnout in nonprofit organizations, and help our team members navigate the often heavy water of trying to save the world, is a thoughtful, disciplined and deliberate approach to addressing the issue at individual, organizational and cultural levels. I don't purport to have all the answers here. I just want to start a discussion. To that end, I'll present a few ideas – and this is by no means an exhaustive or extensively researched list – by directing them toward leaders, organizations and nonprofit funders.

NGO LEADERS

If you are a leader in a nonprofit organization, you have a special responsibility to your team to help them safeguard their emotional and mental health in the workplace. There are three things NGO leaders can do to help their teams avoid burning out: 1) be a model of good decision making; 2) support your team's healthy choices; and 3) don't make it hard.

Be a Good Model

Your first obligation is to yourself. As Jim Butler notes, "Being a good model is key. Your life is your message. Successful activists need bonding from very close people or close groups. It's very important that they have a significant other that they can bond with that gives them that re-inforcement. And to thank others. To extend acknowledgment and appreciation and not to worry about credit and ego but to extend credit to others, empowering others as you go, not worrying about yourself and your own ego."[60]

Are you modelling good, personally sustainable behaviour? Do you create and demonstrate balance in your life? If you leave work at a reasonable time each night, you may notice your team does too. Stay until 8 p.m. and it becomes more difficult for your colleagues to leave before you do.

Being a good model helps; ensuring that people understand the motivation for your decisions is the next step. Share your own story of keeping your boat in the water, or times when you've chosen to eddy out.

Support Your Team

We need to start taking the health of our individuals and teams more seriously. Is there an opportunity for you to lead your team in a way that emphasizes this need?

Individual leadership in the workplace can go a long way. Nearly all of my team at Y2Y took time during the day to exercise, and I encouraged them to prioritize time off, family time and pursuits outside the workplace.

Individual leaders alone, however, can't always turn a boat that is headed into heavy water. It takes a team effort. We need to start walking the talk. That means stressing individual responsibility for setting clear limits on what can and can't be accomplished in the time, and with the resources, available. It also means saying "no," and not fearing the repercussions of this. For leadership, it means being an active advocate for our teammates' limits, identifying them even when they can't and won't, and taking seriously those boundaries once they are established.

This leads naturally into an honest conversation about expectations, both of individuals and organizations. I stress and repeat the word "honest" because frankly I think it's often absent from many of the conversations we have among ourselves in social-profit organizations, and between our partners and funders. We lie, plain and simple.

I've lied to plenty of funders. Some common lies include the following: "Sure, I can still meet these deliverables, even though you're only giving me 60 per cent of the funds I've asked for"; or "Yes, working on this aspect of climate change adaptation is well aligned with my organization's goals and objectives"; and, my favourite, "Sure, I think we can achieve success in the one-year timeline outlined in the grant."

We tell these lies to gain access to money that will keep the doors open and the lights on for our organizations (another reason to consider a sunset clause in all NGO's articles of incorporation). We tell them because we want a seat at the adults' table, where the big conversations are being held. We tell them because we believe that, if we stretch a little, we might actually be able to do what we say we're going to do.

Sometimes we can, and sometimes we can't.

We also lie to one another within our organizations, often right from the start. "Sure, I have time to add this item to my work plan" is a pretty common fib. Of course, we don't have time! We've already committed 125 per cent of our time and this will add another five days we simply don't have! We agree to it in part out of concern for our jobs, in part because we don't want to be left out and in part because we are certain that if we just put in a little extra time now then maybe we'll lick this pressing issue and be able to take a little time off in the spring.

We need to talk with each other about reasonable expectations. Set expectations from the start. Be clear and don't overcommit when there is a risk that you have been asked to do too much. Search for funders who understand this. Don't take money from someone if you don't think you can do the work. And if someone offers you 60 per cent of the requested funds, find a way to scale the work plan accordingly.

Don't Make It Hard

We don't mean to make it hard to stay in the boat, but sometimes we do. There are pressing timelines, deadlines, external and internal pressure to manage, and as leaders sometimes we simply decide that we have to set policies, targets or internal events that may counteract our efforts to support a healthy workplace.

Don't do it.

Easier said than done, but here's the thing: teams notice when we say one thing and do another. If we tell our teammates that we want them to prioritize their own mental and emotional health, and to take responsibility to stay in the boat, and then we make a decision that complicates that effort, it undermines our efforts to support our teams. Make decisions that make reasonable accommodations to your team's efforts to stay healthy.

NONPROFIT ORGANIZATIONS

Nonprofits are by law governed by a board of directors who have, or most often have, two principal mandates: to oversee the organization's financial health, and to hire and/or fire the senior most staff person. In addition, however, most boards of directors also set long-term policy goals for the organizations they lead. Therefore, they have a key role to play in ensuring the CEO, president or executive director of the organization they guide is supported and encouraged to help keep their team healthy and in the boat. Among other things, there are three things they can do: 1) support the leader; 2) insist on effective leave of absence/sabbatical policies; and 3) undertake effective leadership succession planning.

Support the Leader

The most important thing a board of directors can do to help keep the members of its team from burning out is to support the executive director (CEO, president) of the organization to maintain their own mental and emotional health, and that of the rest of the group's staff and volunteers. In providing a team leader with metrics for success, one of the key measurables could be around staff retention and support. How well is the team's leadership supporting a culture that encourages good mental and emotional health, in conjunction with other measurables?[61]

Realistic expectations start at the top. One of the challenges with the save-the-world culture is that we have overwhelming and often unattainable expectations of ourselves, our teams and our organizations. The board of directors sets the long-term direction for the leadership of the organization and, in doing so, creating ambitious but reasonable expectations can help the team's leadership avoid burnout themselves, and encourage a healthy work culture.

Sabbatical Policy

As noted throughout *Taking a Break*, there is an opportunity for organizations to adopt a formal sabbatical policy to allow team members from all levels of an organization to eddy out, scout downriver and revitalize their efforts to navigate the difficult waters of saving the world.

There is strong evidence, based on more than 20 years of research, to indicate the value of a sabbatical policy. "Leaders who are stuck in reactive or even adaptive leadership mode have a chance to refresh themselves and reconnect with their original passion for their cause. They are able to do catalytic generative thinking again," says Deborah Lindell, in a study called *From Creative Disruption to System Change* for the Durfee Foundation. The Durfee Foundation has supported paid sabbaticals for more than 100 nonprofit leaders over the course of 20 years.

The preface to the report states,

> The Durfee Foundation is a private, family philanthropy based in Los Angeles. Since 1997, Durfee has invested in helping to rejuvenate the bodies, minds, and spirits of Los Angeles's most gifted non-profit leaders through their Sabbatical program. Durfee provides time for leaders to break away from daily routines for three months – to rest, travel, explore, learn, and re-connect with family and friends. Central to the Sabbatical program's philosophy is an openhearted belief in leaders and their capacity to both regenerate themselves and become generative leaders for their organizations and communities.[62]

According to Courtney Martin, writing in the *New York Times*, about a dozen US-based foundations have a sabbatical sponsorship program.[63]

Lindell found that the leaders who had taken a Durfee-supported sabbatical reported a wide range of positive impacts on their leadership and their own personal resilience:

- energy for leadership activities;
- work-life balance;
- increased confidence in staff;
- confidence in doing the job.

In addition, Lindell notes in her report that the organizations experienced marked improvements in the following areas:

- culture of the organization is more supportive of work-life balance;
- some or all of the management team jobs are restructured;
- executive director/CEO position is restructured;
- board of directors is more effective;
- organization develops a succession plan;
- sabbatical leave benefit is now available to some or all employees.

The one thing that sabbaticals do not do is result in higher staff turnover: "Sabbaticals do not cause leaders to depart their organizations. Turnover at Durfee Sabbatical organizations is identical to the national average."[64]

That cuts both ways: you won't likely lose a staff person who goes on sabbatical any faster than if they didn't take the time away, but you won't necessarily increase staff retention. The staff you retain, however, will be better leaders, more effective at working with their teams and have a higher quality of life. In short, eddying out will make your team more impactful, with the added benefit of making their lives better. It's a compelling case for the adoption of a sabbatical program and an example of where individual leaders, their organizations and funders can and should work together to support long-term viability of the nonprofit sector.

Succession Planning

At some point, regardless of how well we do these other things, the leaders in our movements are going to want to move on.[65] We need to prepare for that. One of the reasons that many senior leaders stay too long in their roles is that they look around and don't see any realistic leadership succession candidates. This happens because they, and their organizations, haven't planned for succession effectively. Waiting for the organization's CEO or executive director to burn out, retire or die, leaving behind the smoking ashes, isn't an effective leadership transition strategy.

From the very start of a leader's tenure – and here I mean anybody in a position of leadership, not just the top dog – there should be a plan for transition. This is both structural and philosophical in nature. Structurally, leaders should have systems that would allow a new leader to step in on a moment's notice and pick up the ball on organizational and programmatic issues. It's the ol' "if you get run over by a cement mixer on the way to the office, at least we'll know where the budget is kept" argument. If nothing else, it will make it easier to take a vacation or to prepare for the above-noted sabbatical.

From an organizational health perspective, the most important role of any leader is to be cultivating his or her replacements. Creating a pipeline, inside and outside the organization, is critical to creating a culture that supports leaders and their transitions.

The structural part of transition or succession

planning is maybe easier than the philosophical end. Having senior staff regularly update their job descriptions and keeping those on file, effective co-management strategies where senior team members share some of the burden of the CEO or executive director, and the creation of a set of notes prepared and updated by the leader to outline their key responsibilities are internal efforts that can be taken.

Training programs, like the ones offered by Training Resources for the Environmental Community (TREC), are vital to cultivating a leadership pipeline within an organization.[66] Externally, board members and senior staff could always be alert for team members who bring the right cultural fit to the team, and make a point of formalizing this. Quarterly staff meetings might include a discussion about who is in the pipeline and how to get them into your boat.

NGO FUNDERS

By NGO funders, I am principally referring to formal charitable foundations. While government funding is often critical to a nonprofit's bottom line, and generous individual donors are the lifeblood of any development program, my suggestions here are focused on charitable foundations. Here are some suggestions to help your grantees to stay in the boat, and eddy out when needed.

1. Read the recommendation on sabbaticals.

2. Fund people as well as organizations.

3. De-emphasize professional organizations.

Sabbaticals Redux

Read the section addressed to NGO organizations on sabbaticals. Do this. (That was easy, wasn't it?)

Fund People as Well as Organizations

Another important aspect of the relationship between donors and people trying to make the world a better place is who actually receives funding. Charitable foundations must give the vast majority of their donations to charitable organizations, and no money can be given to partisan organizations that do political work. Individuals can give their money to whomever they please, but if they want to benefit from a tax writeoff those dollars must also go to an organization legally allowed to offer a charitable receipt.

It's a perfectly reasonable proposition, except it doesn't always work.

Organizations – be they NGOs, charitable foundations, businesses or even governments – are things we create to do together that which we can't do alone. They most often work well, despite some of the challenges I've outlined elsewhere.

But sometimes the perpetuation of the organization overtakes its mission to save the world. We've all heard of the charitable organizations that spend 60 – 80 per cent of their budget on fundraising, marketing and publicity, and just a small fraction on programs. It could be argued that this is a good return on investment for donors because that high ratio of dollars spent on raising more money allows the organization to continue to do its work.

I disagree. The proliferation of professional charities that spend millions on PR and fundraising undermines the good work the social-profit sector is attempting, creates high-pressure traps that demoralize people who are doing the programmatic work and creates intense stress and anxiety among leaders who are managing these organizations. One way of skirting this problem is to invest in people, not organizations. There are funders who do this, but they still require that funds be donated to a host organization that serves as the individual's employer.

If we developed structures that allowed funders to invest in talented people with the right training and support, this might ultimately solve the problems that vex us today. Organizations will come and go, and they serve a valid purpose, but often they are distractions from the good work we are trying to do. We need to find a way to fund people, on their own or in teams, to do more world-saving work and less organizational-building business. In many sectors of civil society, funding individuals and small, low-overhead organizations would be a much better investment from a cost-benefit ratio, and would allow leaders the flexibility they need to problem solve, organize and motivate at the grassroots level.

Having said that, individuals cannot respond to an earthquake in Haiti, or address massive humanitarian issues that plague nearly every corner of the world. Small organizations can do some good in a localized environment here, but really the big aid groups are needed to address the scale of the challenge.

De-Professionalization

Some have argued that the professionalization of the humanitarian, environmental and social justice movements was the start of a decline in their effectiveness and the resilience of their leadership. I agree but would add that this professionalization was inevitable given the scope of the challenges we face and the lack of leadership from the corporate and governmental sectors.

In the absence of government playing its role in protecting the environment or addressing famine or homelessness, citizens had to step forward. For centuries, volunteers have done much of this work. The first charities were religious organizations such as churches, temples and mosques. During the Enlightenment, the first public charities began to evolve, beginning with the Foundling Hospital, established in 1741 by Thomas Coram. The Foundling was established to attend to homeless orphans living in poverty. In 1756 Jonas Hanway created the Marine Society to attend to the needs of retired seafarers.

As charitable work became more complex, and far-reaching, and as the organizations that supported these efforts grew into major corporations, professionalization was needed to operate them. Now even the smallest watershed societies and human rights organizations have executive directors or CEOs. The work they do is far too complex and much too heavy a load for just volunteers to bear.

One of the corollaries that has accompanied this professionalization, however, has been the need for professional-scale funding. It's no longer possible to hold a bake sale at Christmas and expect it to carry an organization's expenses throughout the year. Fortunately, the level of charitable giving has grown right along with the growth of the charitable sector. And while this might be a chicken and the egg argument, that debate isn't the focus of this work.

What are the expectations that come along with the large-scale charitable giving that drives the finances of most social-profit organizations, and the toll that takes on the organization's leadership?

There will always be a need for professionally run NGOs. The scale of our challenges worldwide is massive, and at times and in places the efforts of huge nonprofit organizations like Save the Children or the Red Cross will be needed. More emphasis, however, should be placed on supporting individuals, small groups, grassroots organizations and networks or community organizations.

Organizations run the risk of becoming more focused on sustaining their own status and, in doing so, creating a disconnect between their purpose and the work their staff and volunteers are doing. Encouraging a broader array of small, medium and large organizations to tackle problems at multiple scales might be one solution.

One way of doing this is to create a sunset or renewal clause in an organization's articles of incorporation or bylaws. After a reasonable period of time – ten years – organizations could examine if they are still needed. This is particularly true of many small grassroots groups that form to tackle a single challenge and then slowly professionalize after that issue has been addressed.

Notes on Technique:
Rescue Mid-River

1. If you're going to attempt a mid-river rescue, your first responsibility is to yourself. Don't upend your own boat trying to rescue someone else; it doesn't help either party.

2. Does your organization need to professionalize? Do you need to hire staff, fund an office and create a donor program? Or is your work done and can you move on?

3. Can we find a way to fund people who are doing good work, and not just their organizations, the latter of which places the emphasis on institutional development rather than policy outcomes?

4. It's time to take our commitment to supporting the well-being of our teams seriously. Hypocrisy is rife in this area and must be the responsibility of all team members to address.

5. What can you do to start paving the way for the next leaders of your team on the day you take over as leader?

Chapter 10

Eddy Back In

My return to the world of social change began in late November 2018 when I started canvassing for Alberta's NDP in the Banff-Kananaskis riding. In the dark nights leading up to Christmas I helped organize door knocking in Canmore. It was a warm autumn and easy to spend a few hours a night knocking on my neighbours' doors for my NDP candidate. In January the local constituency association hired me as the election readiness co-ordinator, and when the writ was dropped for the general election on March 19, I was appointed campaign manager for Banff-Kananaskis.

I'm not going to dwell on the day-to-day activities of this short-term position here. It's a story for another book.[67] What I can say, however, is that the work was by far the most intense of my career and tested my commitment and steadfastness in ways that were both exciting and demanding. During the election, I worked nearly 100 hours each week for a month to support a superb candidate, a phenomenal premier, more than 200 volunteers and a core team of a dozen workers.

I learned as much in those four months of work during the election as I've learned in four years at any other job. Some of those lessons were tactical and involved how to better organize people, campaigns and resources in a political setting; many of these will be of great benefit as I look to lead future undertakings in Alberta, across Canada and North America in the areas of social change. Others were critical to test by fire my ability to work in a highly stressful environment, create opportunities for volunteers and workers to emerge as leaders themselves and advance important public policy issues during the election campaign.

The most important thing I learned was that I was pretty good at being a campaign manager, and that I still had a lot of work to do to make any kind of cause-related work, including politics, sustainable for myself and my family. You can do just about anything when you know your job comes to an abrupt halt – win or lose – on election night. And I did. I believe I may still need some additional effort to do this in a way that isn't harmful to my well-being and that of others around me.

When the election was over, I went back to taking pictures and writing stories but with one noticeable difference: my sense of self-worth was bolstered by the campaign. A lot of the things I'd been told I did very poorly in the past I had able to address in my short-term role with the campaign.

Since that time, I've come to a couple of realizations that are a little surprising. First, when I look back at the pattern of the last year, I see that I've spent much of this time trying to find a way back into the environmental movement in Alberta and in Canada. I don't know now if there is a way back in. There may be, but for now I may have to remain on the outside and focus on other ways of making the world a better place.

The second insight is a little less optimistic but maybe a little more pragmatic: there are many ways to save the world, and struggling within a cause-based nonprofit is only one of them, and maybe not the one for everybody. Nor is it necessarily something that people would want to do for their entire careers, which is possibly why people move between business, government and nonprofit organizations throughout their work lives. The important thing here is to know that, despite how long you decide to rest in the eddy, there are many ways to nose back into the river.

A couple of things will happen when you are back in balance to let you know you are in a good place. Things will seem easy, and everything will seem to flow effortlessly. Obstacles that once presented themselves as nearly insurmountable will fall away without much effort.

Will things get difficult again? Yes, they will. But there is another eddy just downstream. You can hopscotch between them, making a sport of cutting the eddy line. You can rest a few hours, or a day or two, or take a year or more to see how the world looks from quiet waters, out of the fray of the rapids and big water.

We all know that around the bend in the river there are hazards we can't foresee. It's a new river, after all. But after some time, we are ready to paddle again.

In learning to eddy out, we can find some ongoing solace. We don't have to paddle the river in one continuous session. We can eddy hop, making our way downstream, delighting in the joy of finding places to rest and reflect and marvel at the gift that life as people who create change can bring.

Notes on Technique:
Eddy Back In

1. Nose your boat upstream, following the flow of the backwater. Angle the bow at a 45-degree angle so when you cut the eddy fence, the bow will swing around into the flow. The paddler in the fore of the boat should have their blade on the downriver side of the boat and be prepared to draw hard to steady the canoe as it swings into the river. The paddler in the stern steers the course. I've dumped boats doing this when entering particularly fast-moving waters.

2. Eddy back in when you're ready. Don't rush. The river – the world of social-profit activism – will still be there when you're ready.

3. You don't have to eddy back in at all. You can portage around a rapid, or even decide that it's time to try different waters.

4. You are on a great journey. Enjoy it. Make the most of it. Love yourself and others. It is a gift to be alive, and capable of creating positive change, however grand or humble.

Gratitude

First and foremost, my sincere thanks to my wife Jennifer Hoffman, who encouraged me to eddy out and helped me steady the boat while I was on shore scouting downriver, and is invaluable as a source of motivation for cutting back onto the river.

Ed Whittingham, Gareth Thomson, David Thomson (of TREC), Kendall Flint and Michael Jamison served as my informal board of directors during the process leading up to and after my termination at Y2Y and have helped me develop much needed perspective on this and other transformational moments in my life.

My sons Rio and Silas have been among my greatest counsellors, teaching me every single day of my life what it means to live with meaning and courage, while encouraging me to find a line through rough waters that didn't hurt me or those I love.

Several people provided editorial guidance for *Taking a Break* including Cam Westhead, Jim Stelfox and Alaine Kowal. My deep gratitude goes out to them for their sage advice.

Don Gorman at Rocky Mountain Books first encouraged this book in November 2018, exactly when I needed it the most. As usual, Don is a patient and visionary publisher and has been this writer's most dedicated advocate. Thanks to the entire RMB team for putting their backs into this project.

And, finally, to the Belly River, without which I would know nearly nothing of life.

Notes

1 I've been saying this for a long time, and I'm not sure whom this quote can be attributed to. Of course, I used "the Google" and it came up blank. While I doubt it very much, it's possible I said it and just don't remember.

2 Throughout this short book, I'll refer to "saving the world." Nearly everybody who works in or volunteers for the NGO (nongovernmental organization) sector is doing so because they want to make the world a better place. Some do it at the national or international level, nurses and doctors being deployed by Médecins Sans Frontières, for example. Others sit on the boards of their local community associations. Regardless of the scale, we all believe we are trying to save the world, our world, whether it's at the neighbourhood level or on a global scale.

3 When doing the research for *Taking a Break from Saving the World*, I was encouraged to shift to the more positive "maintaining resilience" rather than "burning out." I'll alternate my wording throughout the text but want to emphasize that plain speak trumps framing for me in this small volume.

4 This is a major gap in the research into, and advocacy for, strong mental health in the nonprofit sector and could be the focus of future collaborative efforts between funders and nonprofits themselves.

5 Jim Butler, "How to Effectively Defend the Earth While Maintaining Your Optimism, Energy, Sanity, Sense of Humour, Family, and Keep Your Own Dog from Growling at You" (presentation, "Connections" conference,

Yellowstone to Yukon Conservation Initiative, Waterton Lakes National Park, September 1997). Dr. Butler is professor emeritus of Parks, Forestry and Conservation Biology at the University of Alberta, and is an ordained Buddhist Monk.

6 John Eligon, "They Push. They Protest. And Many Activists, Privately, Suffer as a Result," *New York Times*, March 26, 2018, https://www.nytimes.com/2018/03/26/us/they-push-they-protest-and-many-activists-privately-suffer-as-a-result.html.

7 Bill McKibben, "Money Is the Oxygen on Which the Fire of Global Warming Burns," *New Yorker*, September 17, 2019, https://www.newyorker.com/news/daily-comment/money-is-the-oxygen-on-which-the-fire-of-global-warming-burns.

8 I will use nonprofit organization, NGO and social-profit organization interchangeably throughout this manifesto to represent organizations, large or small, that are undertaking efforts to make the world a better place.

9 Society for Human Resource Management, *2016 Human Capital Benchmarking Report* (November 2016), https://www.shrm.org/hr-today/trends-and-forecasting/research-and-surveys/pages/2016-human-capital-report.aspx.

10 Tracy Vanderneck, "Does the Non-profit Industry Have an Employment Problem?" *NonProfitPro*, May 18, 2017, https://www.nonprofitpro.com/post/nonprofit-industry-employment-problem/.

11 Andy Levy-Ajzenkopf, "Career Burnout: Dodging the Stress Bullet," *Charity Village*, March 10, 2008, https://charityvillage.com/cms/content/topic/career_burnout_dodging_the_stress_bullet/last/137#.XdclM62ZOi4.

12 Sheryl Kraft, "Companies Are Facing an Employee Burnout Crisis," *CNBC*, August 14, 2018, https://www.cnbc.com/2018/08/14/5-ways-workers-can-avoid-employee-burnout.html.

13 Ella Nilsen, "The New Face of Climate Activism Is Young, Angry – and Effective," *Vox*, September 17, 2019, https://www.vox.com/the-highlight/2019/9/10/20847401/sunrise-movement-climate-change-activist-millennials-global-warming.

14 Butler, "How to Effectively Defend the Earth."

15 Chelsea Newhouse, "New Report: Nonprofits – America's Third Largest Workforce," Johns Hopkins Centre for Civil Society Studies, Nonprofit Economic Data Project, May 2, 2018, https://ccss.jhu.edu/2015-np-employment-report/.

16 Michael H. Hall et al., *The Canadian Non-profit and Voluntary Sector in Comparative Perspective* (Toronto: Imagine Canada, 2005), http://sectorsource.ca/sites/default/files/resources/files/jhu_report_en.pdf.

17 There was more to it than that. I was an outspoken advocate for national parks conservation, something I believed was at odds with the management philosophy of Parks at that time. I also didn't respect the lines between my work for Parks – I was a summer park interpreter – and my advocacy, something which was a mistake that I'd change if I had the chance.

18 Again, there was a lot more to it than that. I wrote about this experience in *Running Toward Stillness* (Calgary: Rocky Mountain Books, 2013).

19 Friedrich Nietzsche, *Beyond Good and Evil: Prelude to a Philosophy of the Future*, trans. and ed. Marion Faber (Oxford: Oxford University Press, 2008), 68.

20 Frances Westley, Brenda Zimmerman, and Michael Quinn Patton, *Getting to Maybe: How the World Is Changed* (Toronto: Vintage Canada, 2006), 99.

21 Butler, "How to Effectively Defend the Earth."

22 Dianne J. Russell, "Avoiding Burnout: Finding Balance for You and the Organization," *The Network*, Winter 2002.

23 Butler, "How to Effectively Defend the Earth."

24 I'll talk more about meditation in the following chapters.

25 A few times in this manifesto I'll suggest working with someone to help hold you accountable. This could be a friend, your life partner, a family member or a colleague. As I'll note throughout, if you do choose a colleague, make sure it's someone you don't supervise or isn't your direct supervisor. This will make the effort less awkward and allow you to be more open and honest.

26 Jim Collins, *Good to Great: Why Some Companies Make the Leap...and Others Don't* (New York: HarperCollins, 2001).

27 Peg Streep, "8 Ways You Can Tell That It's the Right Time to Quit," *Psychology Today*, January 6, 2015, https://www.psychologytoday.com/ca/blog/tech-support/201501/8-ways-you-can-tell-its-the-right-time-quit.

28 Streep, "8 Ways."

29 Jacquelyn Smith, "14 Signs It's Time to Leave Your Job," *Forbes*, September 4, 2013, https://www.forbes.com/sites/jacquelynsmith/2013/09/04/14-signs-its-time-to-leave-your-job/#51eee811da82.

30 Mike Lewis, *When to Jump: If the Job You Have Isn't the Life You Want* (New York: Henry Holt, 2018).

31 Laura McKowen, "Marketing Executive to Writer," in Lewis, *When to Jump*, 49.

32 Seth Godin, *The Dip: A Little Book That Teaches You When to Quit (and When to Stick)* (New York: Portfolio, Penguin Group, 2007), as heard on Audible Books, https://www.audible.ca/pd/The-Dip-Audiobook/B071DY98L2.

33 Godin, 65.

34 Sheryl Sandberg, foreword to Lewis, *When to Jump*, xiv.

35 Refer back to "Making a Plan" on page 44.

36 Lewis, *When to Jump*.

37 I have often commented that nonprofit leaders are very poorly equipped to lead organizations in the voluntary sector and the only people less prepared are everybody else.

38 This would have been around 1988 or 1989, and I recall with some clarity reading the *World Watch Report* that outlined these and other emerging environmental issues.

39 While this short primer might suffice to get you started, consider investigating this line of inquiry more thoroughly. A good reference book is Thich Nhat Hanh's *Anger: Wisdom for Cooling the Flames* (New York: Riverhead Books, 2001).

40 Westley, Zimmerman, and Patton, *Getting to Maybe*.

41 Westley, Zimmerman, and Patton, 94.

42 Stephen Legault, *Carry Tiger to Mountain: The Tao of Activism and Leadership* (Vancouver: Arsenal Pulp Press, 2006).

43 Kat McGowan, "Why We Can't Trust Our Memories," *Discover*, July 23, 2014, https://www.discovermagazine.com/mind/why-we-cant-trust-our-memories.

44 Erika Hayasaki, "How Many of Your Memories Are Fake?" *The Atlantic*, November 18, 2013, https://www.theatlantic.com/health/archive/2013/11/how-many-of-your-memories-are-fake/281558/.

45 This worked out to about $100 per beer. It was money well spent.

46 Rudyard Kipling, *Something of Myself, for My Friends Known and Unknown* (Adelaide, Australia: eBooks@Adelaide, University of Adelaide Library, 1937), https://ebooks.adelaide.edu.au/k/kipling/rudyard/something/index.html.

47 Mary Oliver, "The Summer Day," in *New and Selected Poems, Volume One* (Boston: Beacon Press, 1992), 94.

48 Leo Rosten, "On Finding Truth: Abandon the Strait Jacket of Conformity," text of an address at the National Book Awards in New York, *The Sunday Star* (*Evening Star*), April 8, 1962, sec. E.

49 It's occurred to me that, at 20, I was simply a vessel waiting to be filled with whatever theories I heard on a given day. That's possible. But my teenaged years were a little rough, so I tend to buy into Dr. Hill's message.

50 I should mention at this point that I've never done any of these things.

51 Some of the best material on this topic can be found on the *Harvard Business Review* website and Forbes.com. They are worth checking out so you can create your own list. As noted, your rights and responsibilities vary from jurisdiction to jurisdiction, so you'll want to check locally in your state or province for these specifics. A lawyer is almost certainly a necessity here.

52 Carl Jung, *Archetypes and the Collective Unconscious*, vol. 9, part 1 of *Collected Works of C. G. Jung* (Princeton: Princeton University Press, 1959).

53 Scott Jeffrey, *A Definitive Guide to Jungian Shadow Work: How to Get to Know and Integrate Your Dark Side*, https://scottjeffrey.com/shadow-work/.

54 Robert Moore and Doug Gillette, *King, Warrior, Magician, Lover: Rediscovering the Archetypes of the Mature Masculine* (New York: Harper Collins, 1990).

55 Jeffrey, *A Definitive Guide to Jungian Shadow Work*.

56 Thomas Merton as quoted in Parker J. Palmer, *The Modern Violence of Over-Work*, October 15, 2014, https://onbeing.org/blog/the-modern-violence-of-over-work/.

57 Westley, Zimmerman, and Patton, *Getting to Maybe*, 125.

58 Stanley Coren, *Sleep Thieves: An Eye-Opening Exploration into the Science and Mysteries of Sleep* (New York: Free Press, 1997).

59 Kahlil Gibran, *The Prophet* (New York: Alfred A. Knopf, 1923), 35.

60 Butler, "How to Effectively Defend the Earth."

61 According to the *2017 Nonprofit Employment Practices Survey*, a project of Nonprofit HR, 81 per cent of nonprofit organizations in the United States lack a staff retention policy. According to the report, "[This is] problematic, because as corporate hiring continues to heat up and social enterprises and purpose-driven businesses continue to grow, mission-driven talent has more options than ever before. If non-profit employers don't put in a concerted effort to retain their top performers, those employees are likely to look elsewhere." See https://www.nonprofithr.com/2017-nep-survey-new/.

62 Deborah Lindell, *From Creative Disruption to System Change*, https://durfee.org/our-programs/sabbatical/.

63 Courtney E. Martin, "When Being Unproductive Saves a Career," *New York Times*, January 18, 2018, https://www.nytimes.com/2018/01/18/opinion/productivity-saving-careers.html.

64 Lindell, *From Creative Disruption to System Change*.

65 In my experience, most leaders in nonprofits change jobs every 5–7 years. Turnover in key leadership positions - executive directors and development/fundraising teams - occurs more frequently, in the range of 2–3 years.

66 In 2003 I was part of a cohort of leaders who undertook TREC's Senior Leadership Program. It was extremely
   helpful. See https://www.trec.org/services/leadership/
   leadership-trainings/slp/.

67 I'd like to write a little book on this experience and call
   it "The Trail: Out of the Wilderness, onto the Campaign
   Trail, and Back Again." Who knows if it will ever see the
   light of day.

Bookshelf

There are myriad other resources available to those seeking a way to take care of themselves while making the world a better place.

While I haven't referenced more than a few passages of it in this book, I strongly recommend *Getting to Maybe: How the World Is Changed*, by Frances Westley, Brenda Zimmerman and Michael Quinn Patton (Vintage Canada, 2006). This is a once-in-a-generation transformational book that examines how social change happens and how we can transform our approach to saving the world.

The Dip: A Little Book That Teaches You When to Quit (and When to Stick) by Seth Godin (Portfolio, 2007) is a great and short book that can help you decide if you are ready for a change.

When to Jump: If the Job You Have Isn't the Life You Want by Mike Lewis (Henry Holt, 2018) is a practical book that has dozens of stories about people who have made a change in their careers, how they did it and why.

Your local library either has, or has access to, dozens of good books on creating a mid-course career change that often address some of the fundamental questions outlined in *Taking a Break*. How do you know it is time, and how do you do it?

Forbes, Harvard Business Review, Monster and many other websites offer practical and succinct advice on what to do if you are considering quitting, or if you've been fired. They are worth a visit.

About the Author

Stephen Legault is an award-winning author and photographer, conservation and political activist, father and husband who lives in Canmore, Alberta. During his career he has contributed to the protection of more than one million hectares of public land and successfully advocated for Canada's national parks and species at risk. He is the author of 15 books, including nine mystery novels and two coffee table books of photography and essays. His book, *Carry Tiger to Mountain: The Tao of Activism and Leadership*, has been used as a textbook for social change at kitchen tables and in university classrooms.

That all sounds pretty good, doesn't it? He also got himself fired from his most recent full-time job, has burned out, quit a few jobs and generally made a giant mess of things more than once.

That's what qualifies him, as much as can be possible (see "Author's Caution"), to write this book.

He is a lifelong advocate for advocates. He champions people who care for the human condition and the protection of nature, and seeks to serve them as they live fulfilling and rewarding lives making the world a better place.

For more on Stephen's work, or to invite him to speak at your event, visit *www.stephenlegault.com.*